crochet jewellery

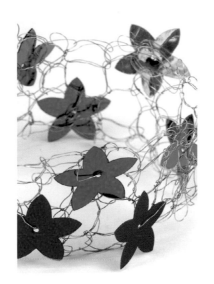

MITCHELL BEAZLEY

Sophie Britten

crochet jewellery

35 fantastic pieces of jewellery to make & wear

crochet jewellery

By Sophie Britten

First published in Great Britain in 2007 by
Mitchell Beazley, an imprint of Octopus Publishing
Group Ltd, 2–4 Heron Quays, London E14 4JP
An Hachette Livre UK Company
Reprinted 2007

ISBN 978 1 84533 255 6

A CIP record of this book is available from the British Library

Set in Syntax LT

Printed and bound in China by Toppan Printing Company Ltd

Senior Executive Editor **Anna Sanderson**
Executive Art Editor **Rhonda Summerbell**
Editor **Sue Whiting**
Proofreader **Naomi Waters**
Photography **Roger Dixon**
Design **Colin Goody**
Production **Faizah Malik**

Contents

introduction

Crochet, knitting, and other home crafts have never been more popular, and crochet jewellery is the latest cool craft that will have you reaching for your hook and making amazing things in no time at all.

Crochet is a wonderful and versatile craft that has been occupying fingers for centuries. It has evolved over time from beautiful and intricate lace-making to a craft that rivals knitting for its suitability for making clothes, and now to a unique way of making jewellery.

Crochet Jewellery is packed full of over 35 original and exciting ideas for all different styles of jewellery at all different levels of skill. Whether you're going for boho chic, high glamour, or sexy sophistication, there are ideas here for every occasion!

As the basis for crochet is a series of chain stitches, it is the ideal medium for making jewellery and perfect for creating necklaces or bracelets; you can even use jewellery wire for a really unusual look. Crochet is also a great way of making flowers and other motifs that can be used as pendants, brooches or on hair slides. There are dozens of different methods using a wide variety of materials, such as conventional wools, sparkly yarns, wire, beads, ribbons, bangles, hair slides, and even curtain rings.

The book includes a fully illustrated how-to section, which will give you all the basics of crochet and jewellery-making, plus useful information on all the materials you might need, and loads of helpful tips.

All the patterns are skill-rated and include easy-to-follow instructions. Most patterns are easy enough for a beginner, with some more challenging and intricate pieces for the more experienced crocheter. However most of the patterns are ingeniously straightforward and many projects can be completed in a couple of hours or less. So for unique hand-made jewellery with a difference, Crochet Jewellery is the perfect book for you. I hope you enjoy making the projects!

materials

Crochet is amazingly versatile. You can use any kind of wire, yarn, string – even strips of fabric – and you can also work in conjunction with a wide variety of other materials, such as rings, bangles, beads, shells, and sequins. In fact, anything that can be crocheted into, or that can be threaded onto the yarn. This book concentrates on wire and yarn and materials that are most suitable for jewellery-making. Here is a comprehensive list of all the materials that you will need to make the projects in this book. More detailed descriptions of jewellery findings and tools are found on page 25.

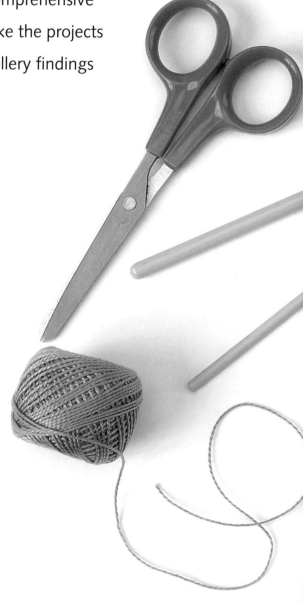

Crochet hooks Hook sizes used in this book vary from 2 mm to 6.5 mm. For tips on choosing the right hook, and a full hook conversion chart, go to page 10.

Tapestry needles Large blunt needles that won't split the yarn are used for sewing in ends.

Sewing needles It is useful to have a collection of different sized needles on hand as these projects use varying thicknesses of thread and yarn.

Tape measure Useful for measuring size and tension.

Small sharp scissors For cutting yarn and fine wire.

Jewellery findings Including clasps, brooch pins, earring hooks. These are available in silver or gold plate and in varying shapes and sizes.

Crimps These are small metal rings that when crushed flat firmly grip a piece of yarn and will therefore hold a bead or clasp in place.

Jump rings Small rings used for joining. These are very useful for making earrings or necklaces and can be used to join the work to an earring hook or clasp.

Pliers Both round-nosed and flat-nosed pliers are very useful jewellery-making tools.

For full instructions on how to use these, go to pages 26–7.

Wire Cutters Fine wire can easily be cut with a pair of scissors. However for thicker wire, more than 0.6 mm, you will need a pair of wire cutters.

Beads These feature very prominently in the book and are widely available in millions of gorgeous hues and in all different shapes and sizes. Bead recommendations are given for each pattern. If you cannot source these exact beads, however, the main thing to check is that the hole is big enough to accommodate the yarn you are using.

Beading needles There are various types of needles used for threading beads. For a full explanation, go to page 27.

Jewellery wire Crocheting with wire is very versatile: it can be worked in simple chains or used to create a fine mesh fabric. It creates a wonderfully unusual and irregular fabric. Take care when working with wire as it cannot be undone as easily as yarn, and overstressing the wire by pulling out stitches may weaken it. More information on wire gauge is found on page 30.

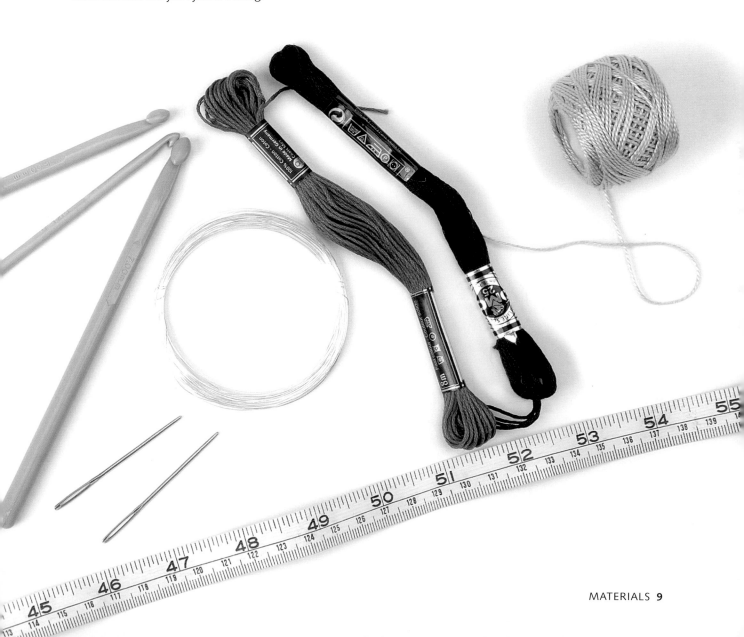

Thick jewellery wire 0.6 mm and 1 mm wire are used in this book to add hold, shape or texture. 0.4 mm wire is used to create pendant beads.

Yarn Recent years have seen an explosion of fabulous multi-coloured, textured, spangly and chunky yarns and there is now a dazzling array to choose from. This book mainly uses fine yarns such as sparkly lurex and lightweight cottons that are perfect for making small pieces such as jewellery.

Glue Indispensable for attaching brooch bars, and other minor jobs. Use a strong glue such as an epoxy or superglue.

Crochet hook conversion chart

Regular crochet hooks vary in size from 2 mm to 15 mm and are 15 cm (6 in) long. They are available in plastic and aluminium with the larger hooks being in lightweight plastic. Crochet hooks are also available in steel. These tend to be much smaller (less than 2 mm), however, and are used for intricate lace-making and filet work.

This book uses metric sizes for the hooks, but you may find that different pattern books use different systems to express the sizes. This chart will help you to choose the right hook. If you find your work is too tight, use a larger hook. Similarly, if it is too loose, you may need to use a smaller hook.

METRIC (mm)	US	UK AND CANADIAN
2.00	-	14
2.25	B/1	13
2.50	-	12
2.75	C/2	-
3.00	-	11
3.25	D/3	10
3.50	E/4	9
3.75	F/5	-
4.00	G/6	8
4.50	7	7
5.00	H/8	6
5.50	I/9	5
6.00	J/10	4
6.50	K/10 1/2	3
7.00	-	2
8.00	L/11	0
9.00	M/13	00
10.00	N/15	000

learning to crochet

Crochet is a fantastic craft and a great creative outlet. It is also an ingenious way of making jewellery. Even the most basic techniques that you will learn over these pages can be used to create stunning and professional-looking jewellery. The great thing about crochet is that, unlike knitting, you work one complete stitch at a time and so avoid the risk of dropping a stitch. This is especially useful when working with fine, fiddly, and otherwise hard-to-see, materials.

The basics of crochet are very simple and once you have mastered the basic action of the hook in one hand, and the control of the yarn in the other, you will be able to make beautiful things in no time.

When you first start off, it is important that you can see what you are doing, and learn to recognize the stitches and their composition. So, for practical purposes, start with a smooth, thickish yarn such as dk (double knitting) or 4-ply in a pale colour and a 4 mm crochet hook.

HOLDING THE HOOK – RIGHT HANDED
Hold the flat part of the hook between the thumb and index finger of your right hand. There are two ways of holding the hook: either like a knife with the end of the hook in the palm of your hand, or like a pen, with the end of your hook over your hand. You should use whichever method you find most comfortable [See below].

HOLDING THE YARN – RIGHT HANDED

The yarn is controlled by your left hand. To control the feed, wrap the yarn from the ball around your little finger, under the third and middle fingers and over your index finger (so the tail end hangs over your palm) [See above]. Extend the index finger to control the yarn and hold the work firmly between the thumb and middle finger. There should be a space of about 5 cm (2 in) between the work and your extended finger [see below].

INSTRUCTIONS FOR LEFT-HANDERS

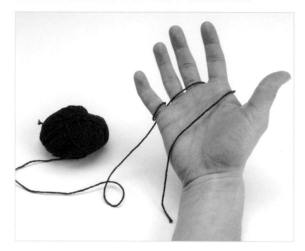

The instructions for crocheting with the left hand are exactly the same as those for the right, except the position of the hook and the yarn is reversed, so left-handers should hold the hook in their left hand and the yarn in their right and reverse the instructions [see above and below]. It may be helpful to prop the book in front of a mirror.

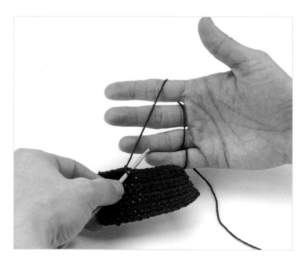

SLIP KNOT

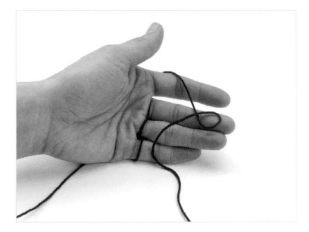

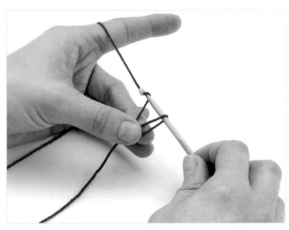

In almost all cases, crochet starts with a slip knot. Leaving a tail of around 15 cm (6 in), (the pattern may say if you should leave more or less), make a loop [See top picture, above]. Now insert the hook into the loop from front to back and draw another loop through it [see lower picture, above]. Pull the knot close to the hook, but not too tight.

CHAIN STITCH (CH)

The first row of crochet is made by working a series of chain stitches (ch). This row is known as the base chain.

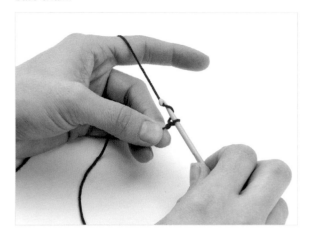

To make a chain, hold the slip knot between the thumb and middle finger of your left hand, keeping the yarn taut, push the hook forward and under the yarn, then over the yarn in a circular motion (this is called yarn round hook, or yrh) [see above].

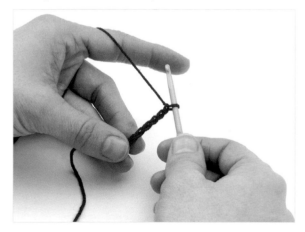

Now draw the yarn through the loop on the hook [see above]. This makes one chain stitch. Take care not to make your work too tight. Each stitch must be large enough for you to be able to comfortably fit the hook into it.

As you make more chains, maintain the tension by keeping a firm grip on your work; this will mean moving the thumb and middle finger of your left hand along the work so that your grip remains close to the hook.

If you are completely new to crochet, practice making chains until you have a smooth action and can easily make even chains of the same size. This is a good way of getting used to the feel of the hook and the yarn.

Once you have mastered this very simple and basic crochet technique you are ready to make a surprising range of beautiful and classically elegant jewellery. These chain necklaces are very quick to make and even a complete beginner can achieve fantastic results.

Above: This necklace is composed of fine silver jewellery wire and amethyst chips worked in strands of crochet chains. This shows how the crochet chains create a unique take on a conventional jewellery chain. The wonderful thing about crochet is how easily beads or gems can be incorporated into the work.

These two projects give you an idea of the diverse effects this very simply technique can have and its ideal suitability to jewellery-making.

Above: This necklace uses a fine yarn threaded with azure glass beads worked in evenly spaced clusters along a strand of chain stitches.

basic stitches

These are the first stitches that you will use in crochet. They are also the most useful, and a basis for many variations. These stitches all use the same basic technique, the key difference being their heights. You will often use these stitches in combination with one another as working with stitches of different heights allows you to create all kinds of wonderful shapes and patterns, and is an essential tool for making motifs such as flowers.

DOUBLE CROCHET (DC)

This is the simplest and most common fabric-making stitch. This is a very easy stitch to make and will soon seem like second nature. As the simplest stitch, it is ideal for making wire mesh as it doesn't overwork the wire. When worked with yarn it creates a compact fabric.

Insert the hook into the next stitch from front to back [see above], (or second chain from the hook if you are starting from the base chain), yarn round

hook, draw the hook towards you through the fabric, yarn round hook and draw the hook through both loops on the hook [see above]. You are left with one loop on the hook. This is one double crochet. Repeat into the next stitch or chain. Work until the very last stitch or chain. This is one row of double crochet.

At the end of the row, turn the work, now make one chain stitch – this is your turning chain – and work one dc into the top of each stitch in the previous row, working from left to right and ensuring that you insert the hook under both loops of the stitch you are crocheting into.

HALF TREBLE (HTR)

This stitch is slightly taller than double crochet. Wrap the yarn round hook before inserting the hook into the next stitch [see above] (or third chain from the hook), yarn round hook, draw the hook through the work, yarn round hook, draw the hook through all three loops on the hook [see below], leaving just one loop on the hook. This is one half treble.

When you reach the end of the row, turn the work, make two chains and continue, working the first htr into the top of the last st of the previous row. Continue to work 1htr into each stitch of the previous row, omitting the turning chain at the end.

TREBLE (TR)

This stitch is taller yet. As with htr, start by wrapping the yarn around the hook and insert the hook into the next stitch (or fourth chain from the hook), yarn round hook, draw the hook through the work, yarn round hook, draw the hook through the first two loops on the hook, yarn round hook [see above], draw the hook through the remaining two loops on the hook [see below], leaving just one loop on the hook. This is one treble.

When you reach the end of the row, turn the work, make three chains to count as the first stitch of the next row. Miss the first treble (last treble of the previous row) and insert hook into the second stitch of the new row. Continue to work until the end of the row, inserting the last treble into the top of the turning chain of the row below.

DOUBLE TREBLE

This is taller than treble stitch and creates a less dense fabric. Wrap the yarn round the hook twice [see above], insert hook into the next stitch (or fifth chain from the hook), yarn round hook, draw the hook through the work, *yarn round hook, draw the hook through two loops; repeat from * twice more until one loop remains on the hook [see below].

TRIPLE TREBLE

Even taller than the double treble stitch, the triple treble is made by wrapping the yarn around the hook three times before inserting it into the next stitch (or sixth chain from hook), yarn round hook, draw the hook through the work, *yarn round hook, draw the hook through two loops; repeat from * three more times until one loop remains on the hook [see above].

SLIP STITCH (SS)

This is the shortest stitch and is mostly used for joining or shaping. Insert the hook into a stitch or chain (always remember to insert the hook under both strands of the stitch), yarn round hook; draw the hook through the fabric and the loop on the hook [see above]. You are left with just one loop on the hook. This is one slip stitch.

making fabric

Crochet fabric starts with a base chain – a series of chain stitches – and can be worked in any given stitch from right to left in rows.

The two keys things to know when making fabric are where to place the first stitch of the first row, and how many turning chains a particular stitch requires. The requirements for each stitch are given below.

FIRST ROW

Double crochet insert hook into 2nd ch from hook.
Half treble insert hook into 3rd ch from hook.
Treble insert hook into 4th ch from hook.
Double treble insert hook into 5th ch from hook.
Triple treble insert hook into 6th ch from hook.

TURNING CHAINS

The number of chains you make at the beginning of a row depends on the height of the stitch, and, except when working in double crochet or half trebles (or where the pattern says otherwise), replaces the first stitch of the new row. Remember: always turn the work in the same direction to avoid twisting your stitches.

Double crochet 1 ch, insert hook into first stitch of new row.

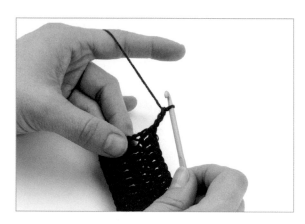

Half treble 2 ch, insert hook into first stitch of new row.

Treble 3 ch, insert hook into second stitch of new row.

Double treble 4 ch, insert hook into second stitch of new row.

Triple treble 5 ch, insert hook into second stitch of new row.

BASIC RULES

After each stitch has been completed there should be just one loop on the hook.

Always insert the hook into stitch from front to back unless you are instructed otherwise.

Always insert the hook under the top two loops of the chain or stitch, unless the stitch or pattern says otherwise.

When counting chains, do not include the loop on the hook, eg if the pattern requires 25 chain stitches, you should have 25 plus the one on the hook.

working in the round

As an alternative to working from right to left, crochet can also be worked in rounds. This is a very useful technique that is used in many of the patterns in this book. It is used to create a circle, as a base for flower motifs, to make 3-D projects such as balls and tubes, and, outside the scope of this book, is an essential technique for hats, bags and other rounded items.

When working in the round, the equivalent to the base chain is a ring. As with flat fabric, start by making a slip knot. To make the ring, make a series of chains and join the last chain to the first with a slip stitch. To make the first round, work the turning ch, then work as many stitches as you need into the centre of the ring and complete the round with a ss into the first ch.

To make a flat disc of concentric rounds, increase by the original number of stitches in each round.

e.g: Make 5ch, join in a ring with a ss.
1st Round 1ch, work 10dc into ring, ss into first dc.
2nd Round 1ch, 2dc into each dc to end, ss into first dc (20 sts).
3rd Round 1ch, *1dc into next dc, 2dc into next dc; repeat from * to end, ss into first dc. (30 sts).
Continue in this way, working an extra 10dc in each round.

Spiral shaping is a quick variation on concentric rounds, but instead of starting and closing each round, each round is a continuation of the last [see above]. You may need to use a marker or a different coloured piece of yarn to show where the round starts and finishes.

Another great use of the round is to make tubes. Make a ring as before, and work as many stitches as you need around it (either into the centre or into each ch). Continue to work in a spiral without increasing or decreasing (see page 21).

tip
Always finish the row or round you are working on when you put your work down to avoid losing your place in the pattern.

tension

This is the number of rows and stitches per centimetre (inch), usually measured over a square of fabric. The tension will determine the size of the finished project. This is obviously of vital importance when making clothes, and less so when making non-fitting items such as jewellery. The most important thing is that your tension is consistent – this will make a nice even fabric. And in the case of earrings, or other items made in pairs, it will ensure that they are both the same size.

When working with wire, the tension can be difficult to control, but this is part of the charm of the medium and an uneven fabric can look more attractive.

To keep your tension even it is a good idea to practice on a piece of scrap crochet to warm up each time you start a project, and in particular if you are going back to a half-completed project.

When using yarn to make bigger pieces of crochet, you need to make a tension swatch to measure your tension. Crochet a square of fabric in the stitch pattern given, making the square at least 10 cm (4 in) in both directions. Measure out the distance stated in the tension and count how many stitches there are within this measurement. If there are too few, your crochet is loose and you need to start again using a smaller size hook. If ther are too many stitches, your crochet is tight and you ned to try again using a larger size hook.

basic techniques

There are an infinite number of variations on the basic stitches that can be used to create all kinds of wonderful shapes and textures. As with knitting, fabric is most often shaped by increasing or decreasing the number of stitches in a row or round. Here are a few basic techniques for shaping crochet.

INCREASING

To increase, simply work one or more extra stitches into the next stitch. A single increase is made by working two stitches into the same stitch. You can, of course, increase by more than one stitch at a time.

DECREASING

To decrease, two or more stitches are worked together. To decrease one stitch in double crochet (**dc2tog**): insert hook into the next st, yarn round hook, draw loop through the work (two loops on the hook), insert hook into the next st, yrh, draw loop through the work, yrh, draw hook through all three loops (see above), leaving just one loop on the hook.

into next st, yrh, draw through a loop, yrh, draw hook through two of the loops on the hook (leaving two loops); repeat this step from * once more, leaving three loops on the hook, yrh, draw the hook through all three loops on the hook [see below].

To decrease by two stitches in double crochet (**dc3tog**), work three stitches together: insert hook into next st, yrh, draw loop through the work, insert hook into next st, yrh, draw loop through the work, insert hook into next st, yrh, draw the hook though the work, yrh and draw the loop through all four loops, leaving just one loop on the hook [see above].

To decrease one stitch in treble crochet (**tr2tog**), work two treble stitches together: * yrh, insert hook

The principal of decreasing is to work the stitch as normal until only two loops remain on the hook, insert the hook into the next stitch, and work the stitch as normal until there are only three loops on the hook; and so on. To complete the decrease: yrh, draw hook through all remaining loops on the hook.

ADDING NEW YARN AND CHANGING COLOUR

None of the patterns require more than one ball of yarn; however you may need to add a new colour. The technique is the same. Change yarns during the last stitch in the row or round by working the last loop of the stitch using the new yarn before you need to change yarn, so the new colour is ready to be used for the turning chain or next stitch.

finishing off

It is very important to take time and care when finishing a project even if you are tempted to rush the final stages. The projects in this book require many different types of finishing, but they all have one thing in common – they will all have ends that need to be sewn in. It is worth doing it right as otherwise you may have an unsightly (and uncomfortable) spike of wire projecting from your necklace, or a stray strand poking through a hair slide.

FASTENING OFF

Cut the yarn, leaving roughly 10 cm (4 in), (if you are going to use the tail to attach a popper or hook, it should be a bit longer). Make one chain, draw the tail through the chain and pull firmly [see above]. Weave in the end an inch or a few centimetres in one direction and then back the other way for a neat and secure finish. Cut off the excess yarn.

You do not need a needle to weave in wire ends as you can weave the wire directly into the fabric, but take care not to distort the shape of the jewellery.

If you are working with yarn, use a blunt-tipped tapestry needle that won't split it.

PRESSING

Occasionally the pattern will instruct you to press the finished item. Place the item under a piece of damp cloth and iron flat. The Goldfingering yarn items will benefit particularly from pressing.

CARE OF FINISHED ITEMS

Wire projects should be handled gently as excessive bending could weaken the wire, which may then eventually break.

Yarn projects should be fairly robust and may be washed. Care instructions for particular yarns should be given on the ball band; however, where there are none or you are unsure, you should wash a sample piece first.

instructions and abbreviations

Crochet patterns use special terms that are often abbreviated or shown as symbols on a chart in order to make the pattern easier to follow. Before you start a project, make sure you understand the instructions and are familiar with all the terms and techniques. A few of the patterns here offer different sizes. To make the pattern easier to follow, go through the pattern before you start, clearly marking which size you are going to make and highlighting all instructions for that size throughout the pattern.

ABBREVIATIONS

This is a list of the most common abbreviations and all those that are used in this book, but is not an exhaustive list as there are many different crochet stitches, not all of which are used here.

Beg	Beginning	**FLO**	Front loop only	**Tch**	Turning chain
BLO	Back loop only	**Foll**	Following	**Tog**	Together
Ch	Chain	**Htr**	Half treble	**Tr**	Treble
Ch sp	Chain space	**In**	Inches	**Trtr**	Triple treble
Cm	Centimetres	**Inc**	Increase	**WS**	Wrong side
Cont	Continue	**Patt**	Pattern	**Yrh**	Yarn round hook
Dc	Double crochet	**Rem**	Remaining	*****	Where there is a recurring instruction, the section to be repeated is marked with an asterisk. Eg: *3tr into next ch sp, 1dc into next dc, 3tr into next ch sp; repeat pattern from * until last st.
Dcb	Double crochet with a bead	**Rep**	Repeat		
Dch	Double chain	**RS**	Right side		
Dec	Decrease	**Sp**	Space		
Dtr	Double treble	**Ss**	Slip stitch		
		St(s)	Stitch(es)		

jewellery-making techniques

The projects in this book use simple jewellery-making techniques that can be easily incorporated into crocheted works. In addition to the usual crochet materials, such as hooks and needles, you will also need some essential jewellery-making tools.

In conventional jewellery-making, there is a huge array of tools and equipment and hundreds of different types of findings available in a wide variety of materials. To keep things simple, only a few key tools are used in these projects. In case you are not already familiar with them, here are some notes on what materials you might need and how they are to be used.

Findings This is a generic term that includes a vast array of jewellery-making accessories such as clasps, earring backs and hooks, brooch bars, rings, jump rings, as well as many other items not used in this book, such as bead tips, spacers, head pins, and so on.

tip
If you don't have a beading needle, or it has disappearing into the carpet, here's a handy tip for threading beads onto yarn or thread.

Cut a piece of wire 7 cm (2 ¾ in) or so long. Fold it over the yarn near the end. Twist one end of the wire a couple of turns very tightly around the other and lay this first end alongside the yarn. Now use the tip of the wire like a needle.

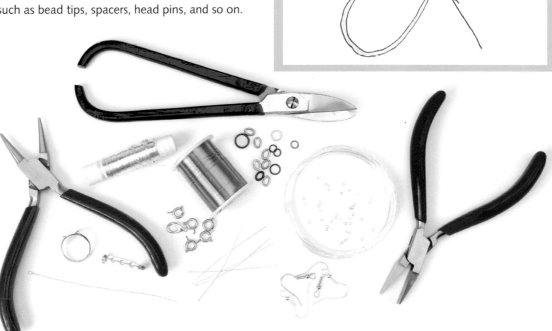

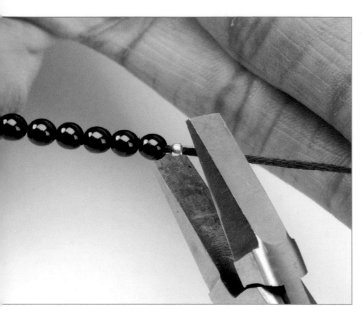

Round-nosed pliers Pliers are absolutely indispensable in jewellery making for taking the fuss out of fiddly jobs. Round-nosed pliers are used for bending wire into a loop [see above].

Crimps Very small metal rings used to finish off a strand of beads. The cord goes through the crimp, through the clasp, and back through the crimp, which is then flattened with a pair of flat-nosed pliers to secure the cord. These are not to be used with wire as the wire will snap when the crimp is crushed [see above].

Head pins These straight pins come in varying lengths and are characterized by a flattened end – this allows you to thread beads onto the pin without them falling off. The beaded pins can be incorporated into all types of jewellery by making a loop at the tail end.

Jump rings Plain wire rings of any size, usually round or oval in shape, used for attaching jewellery parts. These are generally not soldered closed, but can be opened and closed by pushing the ends together. When used with fine wire, seal with a dab of glue on the join.

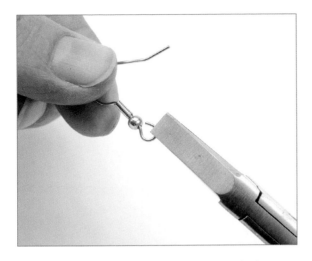

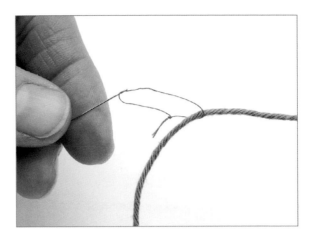

Flat-nosed pliers These are very handy tools that you will use all the time for crushing crimps, opening and closing rings on necklaces, earrings, and other items of jewellery [see above].

Rigid beading needles These are needles in the conventional sense, but they are very slim and the eye is very narrow – too narrow in fact for conventional beading thread, let alone yarn. Make a leader by threading a short length of fine thread through the eye and tying it to create a loop, you can now pass your yarn through this much more ample loop [see above].

Wire cutters A sturdy cutting tool for medium-to-thick wire. Fine-gauge wire can be easily cut using a pair of regular scissors.

Collapsible-eye beading needles A piece of fine-grade steel wire twisted around itself leaving a loop at the top to make an eye. The loop is flexible and is, as its name suggests, collapsible, so that the needle can be pulled through even the smallest bead hole.

beading

There are all sorts of wonderful instruments for beading, such as spinners that allow you to thread beads very quickly and layout boards for designing complicated bead arrangements. However the beading in these patterns is kept fairly simple. Here are a few easy principles to assist you.

When crocheting with beads, you should thread all the beads you will need for the project onto the yarn or wire (while it is still attached to the ball or reel) before you start to crochet. If you are working with large quantities of beads, it is a good idea to add a few more than you think you will need in case you have miscounted. These can be discarded at the end. Thread the beads in the reverse order to the one in which they will be needed (i.e. the beads you need first are threaded last and vice versa).

Always work in good light. Frustration and strained eyes will result from working in the gloom.

Work on a light-coloured towel or fabric surface. This will stop the beads bouncing all over the place if you drop them and you can easily retrieve all the dropped beads at the end.

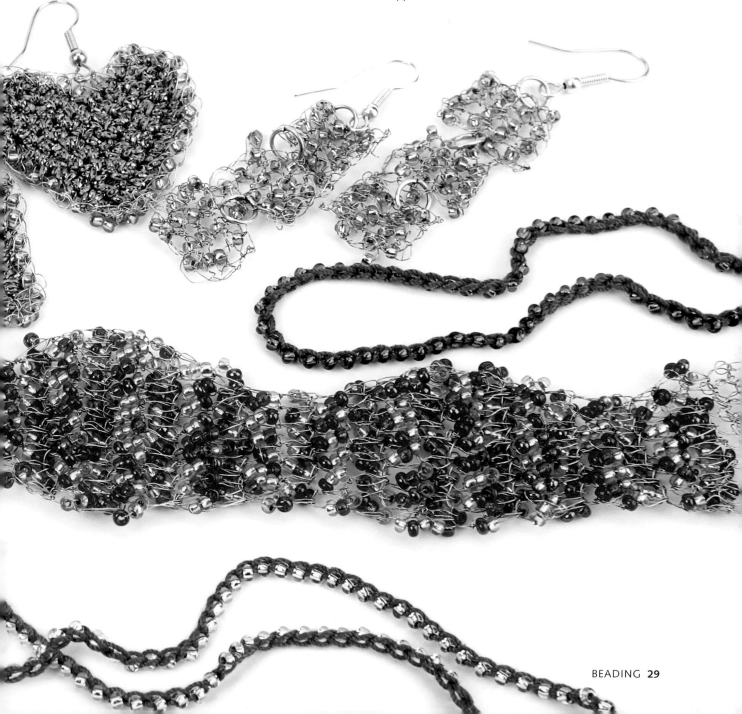

wire

Jewellery wire comes in various gauges and is generally available in silver, copper, and gold colours. You can crochet with any fine wire. In fact the finer the wire, the more flexible it will be and the more fluid your work; conversely, thicker wire may be too stiff and difficult to work with. The wire chart below will help you choose the correct wire. A good tip if you are planning to make a lot of wire projects is to use fuse wire, which can be bought fairly cheaply for a large reel.

WIRE DIAMETER CONVERSION CHART

Gauge	Mm	Inches
32	0.2	0.008
30	0.25	0.010
28	0.32	0.012
26	0.4	0.015
24	0.5	0.020
22	0.6	0.025
20	0.8	0.03
18	1.0	0.04
16	1.2	0.05
15	1.45	0.0571
14	1.63	0.0641

amethyst and wire necklace

Using just chain stitches interspersed with beads and amethyst chips you will be surprised at how quick and easy this necklace is to make. Composed of five beaded strands attached to a clasp at each end, this is a really pretty and professional-looking necklace. A great project for a beginner.

SKILL Easy

MATERIALS
1 reel of 32 gauge silver jewellery wire
25 g of amethyst chip beads
1 tube of Gutermann Rocaille 9 seed beads, shade 1005
Barrel clasp

EQUIPMENT
3.00 mm crochet hook
Scissors

SIZE
One size

PREPARATION
First thread all the beads you will need onto the wire before you start to crochet. Thread one amethyst chip followed by two glass beads until you have a minimum of 54 amethyst chips and 108 seed beads. It doesn't matter whether a strand begins with an amethyst chip or a bead.

tip
You don't need wire cutters for this very fine wire, any ordinary pair of scissors will do.

It is worth threading more beads than you think you will need as you can always discard any you don't use and you will not be able to add more once you have started unless you cut the wire.

PATTERN
Make a slip knot.

This necklace is made very simply by crocheting a series of chains with a bead placed after every second chain.

After every second chain, slide a bead up the wire so that it is close to the last chain you made, make another chain so that the bead is caught in the middle.

When the strand measures approximately 35 cm (13¾ in), cut the wire leaving a 10 cm (4 in) tail and draw the end through the last chain with the hook.

Make four more strands like the first. Don't worry if the strands aren't exactly the same length. Slightly varying lengths will enhance the overall look of the finished necklace.

MAKING UP

Gather all five strands together taking care not to twist them. Attach one half of the barrel clasp to each end by threading the strands through and winding them back on themselves, twisting several times. Cut the ends.

ring o' roses

A very pretty cuff bracelet using both wire and yarn techniques. Dainty yarn rosebuds are attached to a wire mesh bracelet for an arresting yet simple design. Alternatively, use the same rosebud to make a matching hair slide.

SKILL Medium

MATERIALS
1 reel of 32 gauge silver jewellery wire
1 skein of DMC Mouliné 25, shade 321 (scarlet)
Silver popper

EQUIPMENT
2.00 mm crochet hook
2.50 mm crochet hook
Blunt-ended needle
Scissors

SIZES
Small: to fit wrists 15–17 cm (6–6¾ in)
Medium: to fit wrists 17–19 cm (6¾–7½ in)
Large: to fit wrists 19–21 cm (7½–8¼ in)

Instructions for the smallest size are given first, larger sizes are in brackets.

BRACELET
Using the 2.00mm crochet hook and the jewellery wire, make a slip knot, leaving a 10 cm (4 ins) tail. Make 6ch.
1st Row 1dc into 2nd ch from hook, 1dc into each ch to end, turn (5 sts).
2nd Row 1ch, 1dc into each st to end, turn.
Repeat 2nd row until bracelet fits your wrist with 1.5 cm (⅝ in) to spare. Fasten off leaving a 10 cm (4 in) tail.

ROSEBUD
MAKE 5 (6, 6).
The petal effect of the rosebud is created by working outwards in a spiral and then working back into the centre to give the flower texture.

Using the red yarn and the 2.50 mm crochet hook, make a slip knot.
Make 2ch.
1st Round Work 6dc into 2nd ch from hook.
2nd Round 2dc into each dc to end. (12 sts)
3rd Round (1dc into each of next 3dc, 2dc into next dc – 3 times) (15 sts).
4th Round 1dc into each of next 6dc, 1dc around stem of next st, 1dc around stem of next st in row below, 1dc around stem of each of 6 sts in first row. Fasten off and pull tail through so it is now at the back of the bud.

MAKING UP
At each end of the cuff, use the tail of the wire to attach the popper, making sure that you place each half of the popper on opposite sides of the cuff. Weave in the ends to secure.

Ensuring that the rosebuds are evenly spaced on the bracelet, secure each flower by pulling the tails through the mesh with a crochet hook and tying the ends in a knot. Sew the yarn back into the flower and fasten off.

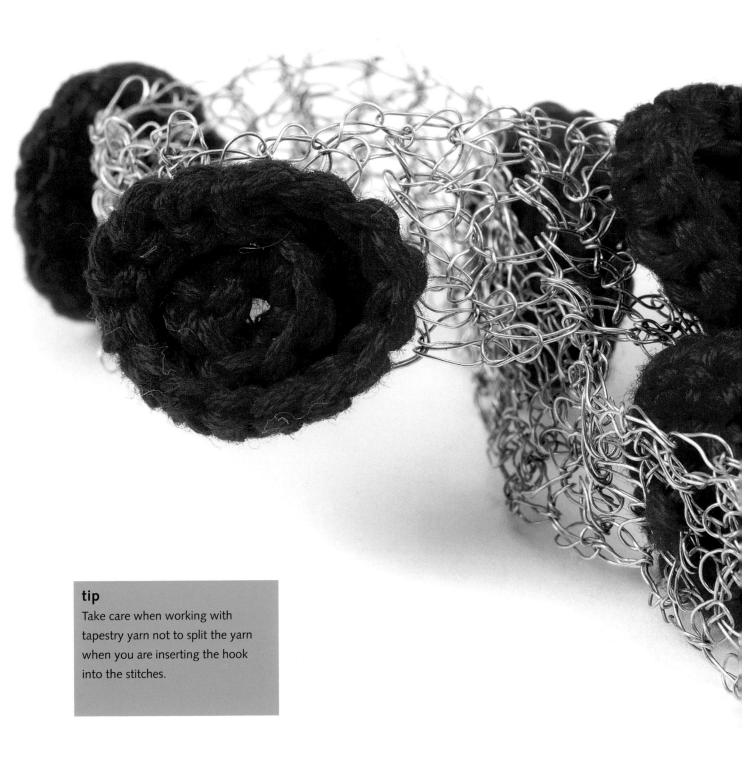

tip
Take care when working with tapestry yarn not to split the yarn when you are inserting the hook into the stitches.

HAIR SLIDE

The tiny rosebuds are ideal for brightening a simple
hair slide. Make a pair of leaves to complete the look.

MATERIALS

1 x skein DMC Mouliné 25, shade 992 (green)

1 x skein DMC Mouliné 25, shade 321 (scarlet)

EQUIPMENT

2.50 mm hook

Blunt-ended needle

Scissors

ROSEBUD

Make 1 rosebud in shade 321 as on page 38.

LEAVES

Using a 2.50 mm hook and shade 992 make a slip
knot. Make 11ch.

1st Row Ss into 2nd ch from hook, 1htr into next ch,
1tr into next ch, 1htr into next ch, 1 ss into each of
next 2ch, 1htr into next ch, 1 tr into next ch, 1 htr into
next ch, ss into last chain. Fasten off.

MAKING UP

Attach the flower to the leaves by drawing the tails from the flower through the leaves and tying in a knot to secure. To attach to a hair slide, simply slide the grip through the centre of the leaves as shown.

super hooper earrings

Create these fantastic dangly earrings in no time at all by crocheting wire and clusters of beads around two different size rings.

SKILL Easy

MATERIALS

2 x 19 mm brass rings (curtain accessories)

2 x 25 mm brass rings

1 reel of 32 gauge silver jewellery wire

1 tube of Gutermann Rocaille 9 seed beads, shade 6510

1 pair of earring hooks

EQUIPMENT

2.00 mm crochet hook

Flat-nosed pliers

Scissors

special term

Dcb This is one double crochet with a bead. To work a bead into the fabric, slide the required number of beads up the wire so they are close to the ring, insert the hook into the ring, yrh, draw through a loop, yrh, draw through two loops. The bead will now be caught in the stitch.

This pattern requires you to add two, three, four, and five beads at a time. This will be described in the pattern as dc2b, dc3b, dc4b, dc5b. These instructions are worked exactly the same as dcb, but sliding more beads up the wire according to the instruction.

BEADING

Thread all the beads onto the wire first. For this project you will need approximately 35 cm (13¾ in) of beads for each earring. It is worth threading a few more beads than you think you will need as you will not be able to add more once you have started, unless you cut the wire.

PATTERN – MAKE 2 EARRINGS

Attach the earring hook to the smaller ring. You may need to use a pair of flat-nosed pliers to manipulate the earring hook.

Without making a slip knot and holding the smaller ring in front of the wire, between the thumb and middle finger of your left hand, insert the hook into the centre of the ring, yrh, draw the loop back through the ring, yrh, draw through the loop on the hook.

Work alternately dc4b, dc2b around the ring, until you have worked 11 sts. This will take you halfway round the smaller ring.

Now you need to add the next ring, so holding the larger ring between the thumb and middle finger of your left hand, insert the hook into the centre of the ring, draw the loop back through the ring, yrh, draw through both loops on the hook.

Work around this ring as with the smaller ring, working alternately dc5b, dc3b [see below], until you have worked 26 sts. This will take you all the way around the larger ring.

Rejoin to the smaller ring by working a ss into the last st you made on the smaller ring (otherwise you will have a gap).

Continue to work around the smaller ring, working alternately dc4b, dc2b until you have worked a further 11 sts. Now join the ring by working a ss into the first st. Cut the wire and weave in the ends.

Make another earring in exactly the same way.

finger crochet bracelets

Easy-peasy necklaces or bracelets with beads made using finger crochet.

SKILL Very easy

All you need is a little bit of wool, some brightly coloured beads and your fingers. It's that simple.

MATERIALS
2 x 120 cm (47¼ in) of dk or four-ply yarn or 120 cm (47¼ in) of ribbon for each bracelet

9 (10, 11) x 1 cm (⅜ in) diameter wooden beads in assorted colours

EQUIPMENT
Collapsible eye beading needle

Scissors

SIZES
Small: to fit wrists 15–17 cm (6–6¾ in)

Medium: to fit wrists 17–19 cm (6¾–7½ in)

Large: to fit wrists 19–21 cm (7½–8¼ in)

Instructions for the smallest size are given first, larger sizes are in brackets.

PATTERN
Take the ends of the yarn from both balls and using a collapsible eye beading needle thread 9 (10, 11) wooden beads. If you are working with lengths of yarn, you will need to secure the beads: holding both strands together tie a knot at one end so the beads don't fall off, then thread the beads onto the yarn.

Wrap the yarn twice around your index finger as shown [see above].

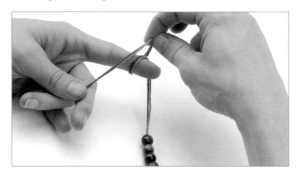

Pull loop 1 (nearest your hand) over loop 2 (nearest your fingertip) and off finger [see above]. You now have one loop remaining on finger which becomes loop 1.

*Using the yarn from the ball, not the tail, wrap one more loop of yarn around finger creating a new loop 2.

Pull loop 1 over new loop 2 and off finger. Tighten the stitches as you go.

Slide a bead up close to the last stitch you made, wrap a loop around your finger creating a new loop 2 [see left] and pull loop 1 over loop 2 and the bead [see lower left].

Repeat from *, adding a bead every other stitch until you have worked all the beads.

MAKING UP

Cut the yarn, leaving a 15 cm (6 in) tail. Draw the end through the final loop and pull tight to secure. Tie the two ends together, ensuring that the bracelet is big enough to pass over your hand and fit around your wrist. Trim excess yarn.

bead and wire amulet

A striking take on the traditional amulet, using bold metallic beads worked into a spiral plate and decorated with beaded fronds, the amulet is then suspended from a silver plated chain.

SKILL Medium

MATERIALS

1 tube of Gutermann Rocaille 9 seed beads, shade 1005 (silver)

1 tube of Gutermann Rocaille 9 seed beads, shade 9625 (dark blue)

1 reel of 32 gauge silver jewellery wire

1 silver plated chain necklace

1 silver jump ring

10 x 5 cm (2 in) head pins

EQUIPMENT

2.50 mm crochet hook

Scissors

Round-nosed pliers

SIZE

One size

special term

Dcb This is one double crochet with a bead. To work a bead into the fabric, slide the bead up the wire so it is close to the fabric, insert hook to the left of the bead into the next stitch, yrh, draw through a loop, yrh, draw through two loops. The bead will now be caught in the stitch.

tip

Double check at each stage that you have got the correct amount of beads. If you have too many beads you can always smash any you don't need with a pair of pliers, but if you have too few you will need to start again.

PREPARATION

Threading the beads. The beads need to be threaded in the reverse order to the one in which they are used in the pattern. This pattern uses simple alternating rings of colour; however, if you want to create a different colour arrangement, chart your work first, and calculate the bead order in advance.

Thread in this order: 48 silver beads, 40 blue beads, 32 silver beads, 24 blue beads, 16 silver beads, 8 blue beads.

PATTERN

Make a slip knot.

Make 5ch, join in a ring with a ss.

1st Round (Right side) work 8dcb into the centre of the ring (8 sts).

2nd Round 2dcb into each dcb of previous round. (16 sts).

3rd Round *1dcb into next st, 2dcb into next st; rep from * to end (24 sts).

4th Round *1dcb into each of next 2 sts, 2dcb into next st; rep from * to end (32 sts).

5th Round *1dcb into each of next 3 sts, 2dcb into next st; rep from * to end (40 sts).

6th Round *1dcb into each of next 4 sts, 2dcb into next st; rep from * to end, ss into first st (48 sts). Fasten off.

DANGLY FRONDS

Thread 25 silver beads onto a 5 cm (2 in) head pin that has a flattened end so that the beads won't slide off. With the right side of the amulet facing, pass the end of the pin through both loops of a perimeter stitch, opposite where you fastened off. Using a pair of round-nosed pliers, and starting at the tip of the pin, make a complete loop [see below].

Continue to add fronds into each stitch along the bottom until you have 10 fronds.

MAKING UP

Attach a jump ring to the centre point at the top of the amulet (the opposite side from the fronds). Pass the chain through it.

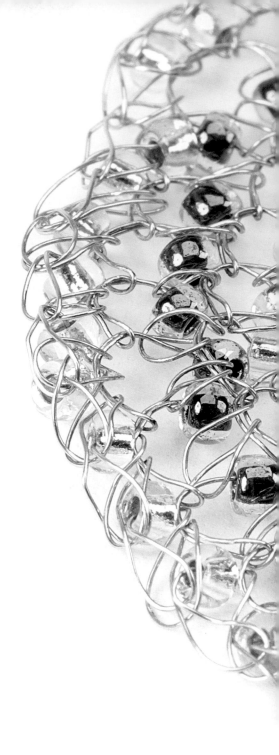

ribbon hair band

An elegant and sparkly hair band, dotted with beads and threaded through with a length of velvet ribbon. Perfect for sophisticated soirées!

SKILL Medium

MATERIALS
1 x 25 g ball of Anchor Arista, shade 340
1 m of 15 mm (⅝ in) width black velvet ribbon
10 g of 4 mm beads
Strong craft glue

EQUIPMENT
2.50 mm crochet hook
Collapsible-eye beading needle
Scissors

SIZE
One size

PATTERN
Make a slip knot.
Make 138 ch.
You are now creating the blocks which provide a frame into which you will weave the ribbon.
1st Row 1dtr into 9th ch from hook, *2ch, miss 2ch, 1dtr into next ch; rep from * to end, turn.
Decorative edging Simple shells worked round the outside give this band a pretty finish.
2nd Row 1ch, ss into first dtr, *4tr in 2ch sp, ss with bead into next dtr; repeat from * to last block. Work 12tr into last block: this will take you round to the other edge of the hairband. Now work 1ss with a bead into base of first dtr. Continue as before to work (4tr in 2ch sp, ss with bead into base of next dtr) until you reach the last block. Work 8tr

special terms
Dtr (double treble) Wrap the yarn round the hook twice, insert hook into the work, yrh, draw a loop through the work, yrh, draw through first two loops on hook, yrh, draw through the next two loops on the hook, yrh, draw through the last two loops on the hook. You will be left with one loop on the hook.

Slip stitch with a bead Slide the bead up yarn so it is close to the fabric, insert hook to the left of the bead and into next stitch, yrh, draw the hook through the fabric and the loop on the hook.

into last block, finishing with a ss into top of 1st dtr. Fasten off.

MAKING UP

Starting from the back, thread the velvet ribbon through the hair band. Finish the ribbon by folding the ends in half and making a cut as shown, open the ribbon up and seal the ends with glue or clear nail varnish. Sew in all ends.

tip
To stop your ribbon unravelling from the reel when you stow it, secure the end with a pin.

foxy fire choker

Create this amazing-looking choker just by working silver wire in double crochet, incorporating hundreds of fiery beads of different shades. The choker is finished off with a hook-and-eye fastening.

SKILL Medium

MATERIALS

1 tube of Gutermann Rocaille 9 seed beads, shades 1850, 3565, 1245, and 4740

1 reel of 32 gauge silver jewellery wire

2 pairs of No.1 silver hooks and eyes

EQUIPMENT

2.50 mm crochet hook

Scissors

SIZE

This choker can be made to any size; measure against your neck as you go.

special terms

Dcb This is one double crochet with a bead. To work a bead into the fabric: slide the bead up the wire so it is close to the fabric, insert hook to the left of the bead into the next st, yrh, draw through a loop, yrh, draw through two loops. The bead will now be caught in the stitch.

Dc3b This is the same as dcb, except you add three beads at a time.

Dcb2tog A decrease of one stitch by working two stitches together, adding just one bead: slide the bead up to the last st worked, insert hook to the left of the bead and into the next st, yrh, draw through a loop, insert hook into next st, yrh, draw through a loop, yrh, draw through all three loops on hook, leaving just one loop [see left].

In this pattern as you are adding three beads to each stitch, the pattern instruction will read dc3b2tog, where only three beads are added across both stitches.

2dc3b An increase of one stitch by working 2dc into one stitch, adding three beads with each dc.

PREPARATION

Thread all the beads onto the wire first. To complete this project you will need approximately 275 cm (108 in) of beads; this will be ample for any size.

PATTERN

Make a slip knot leaving a 20 cm (8 ins) tail.
Make 11ch.

1st Row 1dc into 2nd ch from hook, 1dc into each ch to end, turn. (10 sts)

2nd Row 1ch, 1dc into each dc to end, turn.
Repeat 2nd row twice more.

This is just a guideline. This choker has a natural flowing look so you can follow the pattern or go freestyle, alternately increasing and decreasing at the beginning and end of the row to create a wavy shape.

Choker body

1st Row 1ch, dc3b2tog, 1dc3b into each of next 6 sts, dc3b2tog, turn. (8 sts)

2nd Row 1ch, dc3b2tog, 1dc3b into each of next 4 sts, dc3b2tog, turn. (6 sts)

3rd Row 1ch, 1dc3b into each st to end, turn.

4th Row 1ch, 2dc3b into 1st st, 1dc3b into each st to end, turn. (7 sts)

5th Row 1ch, 1dc3b into each st to last st, 2dc3b into last st, turn. (8 sts)

6th Row 1ch, 1dc3b into each st to last st, 2dc3b into last st, turn. (9 sts)

7th Row 1ch, 2dc3b into 1st st, 1dc3b into each st to end, turn (10 sts).

8th Row 1ch, 2dc3b into 1st st, 1dcb into each st to last st, 2dc3b into last st (12 sts).

9th Row 1ch, 1dc3b into each st to end, turn.

10th Row 1ch, dc3b2tog, 1dc3b into each of next 8 sts, dc3b2tog, turn (10 sts).

Repeat row 1–10 of the pattern until the choker just fits around your neck. Now without adding any beads work four rows straight:

Next Row 1ch, 1dc into each dcb to end, turn.

Next Row 1ch, 1dc into each dc to end, turn.
Repeat this row two more times. Fasten off leaving a long tail.

MAKING UP

Using the long wire tails at each end, attach the hooks and eyes to correspond at each end of the choker. Weave in the ends.

tip

If you are not able to complete the pattern by the time the choker fits nearly around your neck, simply increase or decrease as appropriate until you have 10 sts across, then work four rows of dc so that both ends match.

gold cuff

This elegant cuff looks like a classic piece of jewellery, easy to wear and very quick to make. The design is a simple shell pattern which is held in shape by wire, which is crocheted into the cuff in the last row.

SKILL Medium

MATERIALS

1 x 25 g ball of Twilleys Goldfingering in gold, shade 35

50 cm (19½ in) of 20 gauge jewellery wire

1 gold bugle bead

Strong craft glue

EQUIPMENT

3.00 mm crochet hook

Blunt-ended needle

Scissors

Wire cutters

Pliers – any

SIZE

This cuff can be made to any size. Measure against your wrist as you go.

PATTERN

Make a slip knot.

Make 11ch.

1st Row One shell into 8th ch from hook, miss 2ch, 1dtr into last ch, turn.

2nd Row 5ch, miss 3 sts, 1 shell into next st, miss 2 sts, 1dtr into 4th of 7ch at start of 1st row, turn.

3rd Row 5ch, miss 3 sts, 1 shell into next st, miss 2 sts, 1dtr into 4th of 5ch, turn.

Repeat third row until the cuff fits comfortably around your wrist but with no overlap.

Shell The shell in this pattern is comprised of five complete double trebles which are worked into one stitch to create a shell or fan shape [see above].

Dtr (double treble) Wrap the yarn round the hook twice, insert hook into the work, yrh, draw a loop through the work, yrh, draw through first two loops on hook, yrh, draw through the next two loops on the hook, yrh, draw through the last two loops on the hook. You will be left with one loop on the hook.

1st Round 1 ch, work 1 round of dc evenly around the edges of the cuff as follows: work 4dc into 1st ch sp, *1 dc into next st, 2dc into next ch sp; rep from * to

Before you start to work the wire into your bracelet, fold the ends of the wire over using a pair of pliers, this way the wire is less likely to be drawn into your work as you crochet around the cuff.

last ch sp on first side, 4dc into last ch sp, 3dc into base of shell, 4dc into next ch sp *1dc into next st, 2dc into next ch sp; rep from * until you reach the last ch sp, 4dc into last ch sp, 1dc into each of next 2 sts.
2nd Round Laying the wire alongside your work, 1dc around the wire into each dc to end.

MAKING UP
Trim off any excess wire. Now put a dab of glue onto each end of the wire and insert into either side of a bead to secure. Sew in all ends. You might need to shape the bangle so that it is symmetrical and fits nicely around your wrist.

hippy ring

A sweet flower-power ring made in contrasting sparkly shades. Worked in just two rounds, even a beginner will be able to make this very simple ring quickly.

SKILL Easy

MATERIALS

1 x 25 g ball of Twilleys Goldfingering, shade 60
1 x 25 g ball of Twilleys Goldfingering, shade 35
1 ring base
Strong craft glue

EQUIPMENT

2.00 mm crochet hook
Blunt-ended needle

SIZE

One size

PATTERN

Using shade 60, make a slip knot.
Make 4ch and join in a ring with a ss.
1st Round 1ch, work 8dc into ring, join with a ss into back loop of 1st dc.
2nd Round *3ch, 1 cluster, 3ch, ss blo into same back loop, ss blo into next st; rep from * to end, working last ss into back of 1st dc from 1st round. Fasten off.

Using shade 35, attach yarn to front loop of 1st dc in first round. Work 1dc flo into each stitch in 1st round. Ss flo into 1st dc. Fasten off.

special terms

Flo Front loop only. Work the stitch in the normal way, but inserting the hook under the front loop only of each st.
Blo Back loop only. Work the stitch in the normal way, but inserting the hook under the back loop only of each st.

Cluster This cluster is comprised of three trebles worked into the same stitch, leaving the last loop of each stitch on the hook. When all three trebles have been worked, yrh, and draw through all four loops on the hook.

MAKING UP

Sew in all ends. Place a dab of glue on the ring base and press the flower firmly into place.

diamond life earrings

Elegant wire mesh earrings worked into a diamond shape glittering with silvery beads.

SKILL Medium

MATERIALS

1 tube of Gutermann Rocaille 9 seed beads, shade 1005

1 reel of 32 gauge silver jewellery wire

1 pair of earring hooks

EQUIPMENT

2.00 mm crochet hook

Flat-nosed pliers

Scissors

PREPARATION

First, thread on all of the beads you will need for each earring; if you run out of beads you will need to cut the wire and add some more, so it is always worth adding more than you think you will need. You will need to thread on approximately 13 cm (5 in) of beads (or 75 beads) for each earring.

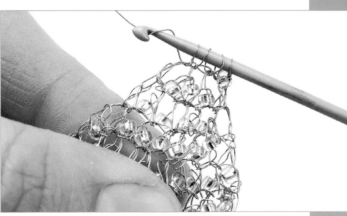

special terms

Dcb This is one double crochet with a bead. To work a bead into the fabric, slide the bead up the wire so it is close to the fabric, insert hook to the left of the bead and into the next stitch, yrh, draw through a loop, yrh, draw through two loops. The bead will now be caught in the stitch.

Dcb2tog A decrease of one st by working two sts together adding just one bead. Slide the bead up to the last st worked, insert the hook into the next st, yrh, draw through a loop, insert the hook into the next st, yrh, draw through a loop, yrh, draw through all three loops on hook, leaving just one loop.

Dcb3tog A decrease of two sts by working three sts together adding just one bead. Slide the bead up to the last st worked, insert the hook into the next st, yrh, draw through a loop, insert the hook into the next st, yrh, draw through a loop, yrh, insert the hook into the next st, yrh, draw through a loop, yrh, draw through all four loops on hook, leaving just one loop [see left].

Note on increasing (working two or more st in the same place): add a bead for each stitch you work, so an increase of one stitch will have two beads.

There is no right or wrong side. As the beads are added to every row, they can be seen equally from both sides.

PATTERN

Starting at the top of the earring, make a slip knot. Make 2ch.

1st Row 1dcb in 2nd ch from hook, turn.

2nd Row 1ch, 3dcb into the st, turn.

3rd Row 1ch, 2dcb into first st, 1dcb into next st, 2dcb into final st, turn (5 sts).

Continue to work in double crochet adding a bead in each st and increasing by one st at each end of every row until there are 11 sts.

Next Row 1ch, 1dcb into each st to end, turn.

Next Row 1ch, dcb2tog, 1dcb into each of next 7 sts, dcb2tog, turn (9 sts).

Continue to work in double crochet adding a bead in each st and decreasing by one st at each end of every row until three sts remain.

Next Row 1ch, dcb3tog, turn.

Next Row 1ch, 1dcb into final st. Fasten off.

MAKING UP

Weave the wire ends into the mesh and cut. Add an earring hook to the top of earring. You may need to use the pliers to open and close the wire loop that attaches to the diamond.

tips

Working with wire can be fiddly, and the wire may not behave in the way that yarn does. You should be familiar with the appearance of crocheted fabric so that you can find the stitches more easily.

Always work under a bright light; it can be hard to see what you are doing with wire.

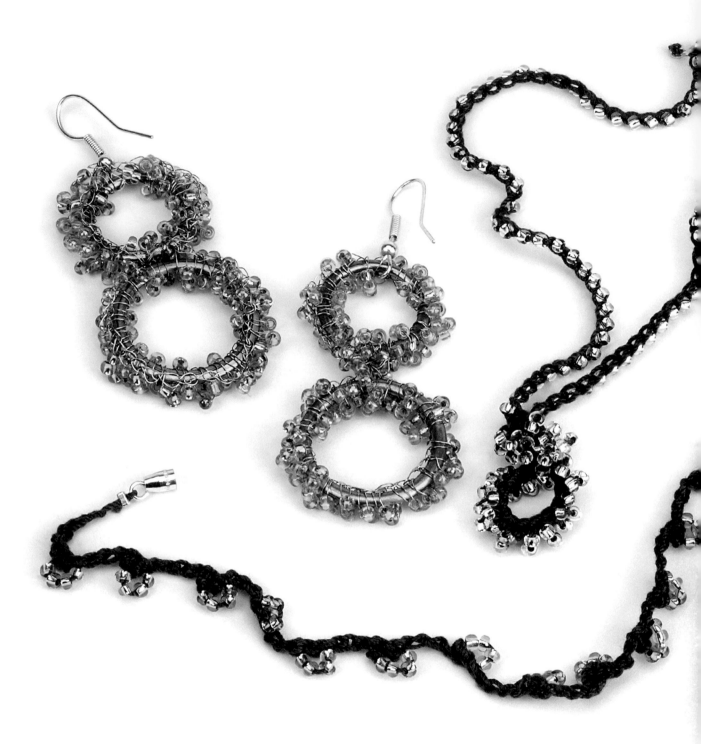

bang bangles

Create cool and unusual bangles in record time. Using any yarn you like – chunky, fine, sparkly, or fluffy – simply crochet around a plain metal bangle. You can make your bangles all the same colour or mix and match with a variety. Each bangle only uses a small amount of yarn, so one ball of yarn will make dozens of bangles. Alternatively, it is a great way of using up odds and ends.

SKILL Easy

MATERIALS
1 x 50 g ball of yarn – **Twilleys Goldfingering yarns:** sea green (shade 66), non-metallic silver (57), sparkly pink (62), sparkly black (31), sparkly purple (60), sparkly light blue (53); **Pink fluffy:** Wendy Jazz in Memphis; **Black:** RYC Cashsoft dk in Black; **Blue wool:** Colinette point 5 in Neptune
4 mm silver beads
Plain metal bangles

EQUIPMENT
Blunt-ended needle
3.00 mm crochet hook
Scissors

SIZE
One size

This is a very simple project – and is made up of just one round of double crochet worked profusely all around the bangle. The trick is in starting off.

PATTERN
Make a slip knot.
Hold the bangle in front of the yarn, between the thumb and middle finger of your left hand. Insert the hook into the ring, wrap the yarn round the hook, draw the loop through the ring, yrh, draw through the loop on the hook [see below].

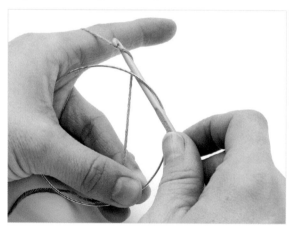

Insert the hook into the ring once more, yrh, draw loop through the ring, yrh, draw hook through both loops on the hook – this will leave one loop. This makes one double crochet.

Continue to work around the bangle in double crochet until you have worked as many stitches as you can fit in. This will make the yarn twist and buckle to give it a wavy look. You may need to keep bunching up the stitches you have made to create more room.

Beaded bangles

For an original twist why not add beads to your bangle? Thread all the beads for the project in advance and add one bead after every few stitches. In the bangle shown below right, a bead was added to every fourth stitch with the dcb technique (see page 42), using a total of 30 beads.

MAKING UP

Fasten off by cutting the yarn, making one chain then drawing the tail through the chain. Now pull tight. Sew in the ends. Arrange the yarn so that it is twisted evenly around the bangle.

simple bead necklaces

These sweet necklaces couldn't be simpler to make and are an ideal project for a complete beginner. Just by following a few simple steps you can create beautiful jewellery in literally minutes!

SKILL Very easy

MATERIALS

1 tube of Gutermann Rocaille 9 seed beads, shades 7300, 7230 and 1005

1 x 50g ball of DMC Babylo 10/8 crochet yarn, shade 482

2 crimps per necklace

1 barrel clasp per necklace

EQUIPMENT

2.50 mm crochet hook

Flat-nosed pliers

Collapsible-eye beading needle

Scissors

SIZE

These can be made to any size; measure against your neck as you go.

BEAD CHAIN

This is the most straightforward bead necklace; it is simply a chain of crochet, with a bead after each stitch. Try to make nice even stitches; it will help to keep your work quite tight.

Using bead shade 7300, thread approximately 150 beads onto the yarn (this is about 25 cm, 9¾ in, of beads) using the beading needle. This will be enough beads for any size. It is important you thread all the beads you will need (and a few more just in case)

before you start making your necklace. To add more you would need to cut the yarn which would spoil the look of this simple chain.

MAKE A SLIP KNOT

Make a loop near the end of the yarn, leaving a 10 cm (4 in) tail) now insert the hook into the loop from front to back and draw another loop through it. Pull the knot close to the hook, but not too tight.

MAKING CHAINS

This necklace is made very simply by a series of chains with a bead added after every chain. To make a chain, wrap the yarn round the hook from back to front and draw it through the loop on the hook. This makes one chain stitch.

You might want to practice making a few chains until you have a nice smooth action.

ADDING BEADS

Once you have mastered the chain stitch, you are ready to make your necklace. Slide a bead up the yarn, close to the slip knot, wrap the yarn round the hook, and draw it through the loop on the hook, making a chain st. Continue in this way, bringing a bead up the yarn, then working a chain stitch until the necklace is long enough to fit comfortably around your neck.

MAKING UP

Cut the yarn leaving a 10 cm (4 ins) tail and draw the end through the last chain.

At each end, using the beading needle, thread on the crimp, then the barrel clasp, now pass the needle back through the crimp. Crush the crimp with the pliers to secure the yarn and cut the yarn off close to the crimp.

PETAL CHAIN

This is a variation on the bead chain. Again, the necklace is worked as just one chain, but instead of inserting a bead into each stitch, you will be making a series of small loops with beads.

Using bead shade 7230, thread on approximately 150 beads – this will be about 25 cm (9¾ in) of beads.

MAKE A SLIP KNOT

Make 6ch. Now slide four beads up the yarn, close to the last st you made, insert the hook into the 3rd ch from the hook (not counting the ch on the hook), wrap the yarn round the hook, draw through a loop, wrap the yarn round the hook, draw through two loops. This is one double crochet.

Continue in this way, working *6ch, adding four beads, then working 1dc into 3rd ch from hook; rep from * until the necklace is long enough to fit comfortably around your neck, ending with 6ch. Finish off as for the bead chain.

PENDANT CHAIN

A very easy way of making a striking pendant necklace using just seed beads and crochet yarn.

Using bead shade 1005, first thread at least 160 beads (this will be about 28 cm, 11 ins, of beads).

MAKE A SLIP KNOT

Slide a bead up to the knot, *1ch, one bead, 1ch; rep from * until you have worked in 50 beads, then work 20 chains without beads. Work a slip stitch into the 20th ch from the hook. Now, adding three beads with each stitch, work 20dc into the centre of the ring. Slip stitch into the first chain. Slide a bead up to the pendant, *1ch, one bead, 1ch; rep from * until you have worked in 50 beads. Fasten off. Finish off as for the bead chain.

stripy bead earrings

Make cool dangly earrings with crocheted balls mixed with beads. You can add as many as you fancy and mix with any beads you like – just remember not to make them too heavy!

SKILL Easy

MATERIALS

DMC Mouliné 25 yarn, shade 125

Small bag of polyester filling or cotton wool

6 x Gutermann 8 mm glass beads in black, shade 1000

4 x Gutermann Rocaille 9 seed beads, shade 7300

1 pair of earring hooks

2 jump rings

EQUIPMENT

2.50 mm hook

Collapsible-eye beading needle

Blunt-ended needle

Sharp needle

Scissors

TENSION

Small balls should measure 2 cm (¾ in) diameter.

Large balls should measure 2.5 cm (1 in) diameter.

It doesn't matter if you don't stick exactly to these measurements, but you want to ensure that you work to the same tension for both earrings otherwise they will look uneven.

tip
Mark the beginning of each round with a piece of coloured thread to avoid losing your place.

SMALL BALL – MAKE 2

Make a slip knot.

Make 2ch.

1st Round Work 8dc into 2nd ch from hook.

2nd Round 2dc into each dc to end (16 sts).

3rd and 4th Rounds 1dc into each dc to end.

Place filling into the ball.

5th Round Dc2tog 8 times. (8 sts)

6th Round 1dc into each dc to end.

Fasten off. Sew in ends.

LARGE BALL – MAKE 2

Make a slip knot.

Make 2ch.

1st Round Work 8dc into 2nd ch from hook.

2nd Round 2dc into each dc to end. (16 sts)

3rd Round *1dc into each of the next 3dc, 2dc into next dc; rep from * to end. (20 sts)

4th Round 1dc into each dc to end.

5th Round As 4th round.

6th Round *1dc into each of next 3dc, dc2tog into next dc; rep from * to end. (16 sts)

7th Round Dc2tog 8 times. (8 sts)

8th Round 1dc into each dc to end.

Fasten off. Sew in ends.

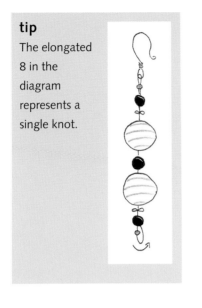

MAKING UP

Cut a 20 cm (8 in) piece of the yarn and thread it onto
a sharp needle (a sharp needle will pass through the
stuffing more easily). Pass it through the smaller of the
two beads. Using the beading needle (assuming the
bead won't pass over the regular needle), thread one
8 mm bead. Again, using the sharp needle thread the
second crochet ball. Now, using the big eye needle,
thread one more 8 mm bead following by one seed
bead. Pass the yarn back through the 8 mm bead and

tie a knot between the larger crochet ball and the
8 mm bead.

Pull the other end of the yarn firmly so that the
balls and the beads are now snug. Thread one 8 mm
bead, one seed bead, and the earring hook, and pull
the yarn firmly so the beads are snug with no gaps
between them. Now pass the yarn back through the
seed bead and 8 mm bead and secure with a knot
between the smaller crochet ball and the 8 mm bead.
Sew in all ends.

bead and mesh cuff bracelets

These pretty cuff bracelets are created using wire worked into a mesh with beads added for decoration. You can add the beads in any design you like by following a simple chart like the one given here, or make up your own.

SKILL Easy

The technique used here is simply double crochet fabric; however, you should be familiar with the appearance of regular yarn fabric before attempting this project as the stitches can be a little hard to identify at first.

MATERIALS

1 reel of 32 gauge silver jewellery wire

1 tube of Gutermann Rocaille 9 seed beads, shade 7300

1 tube of Gutermann Rocaille 9 seed beads, shade 4740

1 tube of Gutermann Facon star sequins, shade 9912

1 silver popper for each cuff (except sequin cuff)

EQUIPMENT

2.50 mm crochet hook (bead cuffs)

6.50 mm crochet hook (sequin cuff)

Scissors

SIZES

Small: to fit wrists 15–17 cm (6–6¾ in)

Medium: to fit wrists 17–19 cm (6¾–7½ in)

Large: to fit wrists 19–21 cm (7½–8¼ in)

Instructions for the smallest size are given first, larger sizes are in brackets.

It is important to note that the beads will be on whichever side you are working, so you might want to add beads only onto the right side of the mesh

special term

Dcb This is one double crochet with a bead. To work a bead into the fabric, slide the bead up the wire so it is close to the fabric, insert hook to the left of the bead and into the next stitch, yrh, draw through a loop, yrh, draw through two loops. The bead will now be caught in the stitch.

BEAD STRIPE BRACELET

Create a stripy pattern by working a row of beads (shade 4740) on every right side row.

You will need approximately 80 (90, 100) beads. Thread these directly onto the wire before you start to crochet.

PATTERN

Using a 2.50 mm hook, make a slip knot, leaving a 10 cm (4 in) tail.

Make 6ch.

1st Row (Right side) 1dc into 2nd ch from hook, 1dc into each ch to end, turn (5 sts).

tip

You may want to add a few more beads in case you have miscounted. Any beads you don't use can be discarded at the end.

2nd Row 1ch, 1dc into each st to end, turn.

3rd and 4th Rows As 2nd row.

Next Row 1ch, 1dcb into each dc to end, turn.

Next Row 1ch, 1dc into each dcb to end, turn.

Repeat last two rows until bracelet just fits around your wrist, then repeat 2nd row four times. Fasten off leaving a 10 cm (4 in) tail.

MAKING UP

At each end, use the tail to attach the popper, making sure that you place each half of the popper on opposite sides of the cuff. Weave in the ends to secure.

BEAD CLUSTER BRACELET

Similar to the stripy design, this time arranging the beads (shade 7300) in clusters of four. A double crochet with four beads worked into it will be described as dc4b.

You will need approximately 112 (124, 136) beads. Thread these onto the wire.

PATTERN

Using a 2.5 mm hook, make a slip knot, leaving a 10 cm (4 in) tail.
Make 6ch.

1st Row 1dc into 2nd ch from hook, 1dc into each ch to end, turn (5 sts).

2nd Row 1ch, 1dc into each st to end, turn.

3rd and 4th Rows As 2nd row.

Next Row 1ch, 1dc into each of next 2dc, 1dc4b into next dc, 1dc into last 2dc, turn.

Next Row 1ch, 1dc into each st to end, turn.

Next Row 1ch, 1dc4b into 1st dc, 1dc into each of next 3dc, 1dc4b into last dc, turn.

Next Row 1ch, 1dc into each st to end, turn.

Repeat the last 4 rows until bracelet just fits around your wrist, then repeat row 2 four times. Fasten off leaving a 10 cm (4 in) tail.

See bead stripe bracelet for notes on making up.

CHARTS

You can create a bead chart like the one below. You might find this easier to follow than a pattern. This is the chart for the bead cluster bracelet.

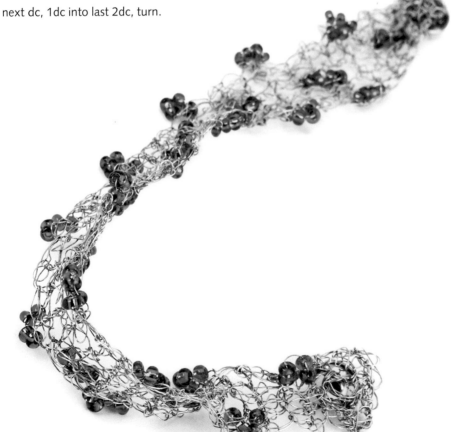

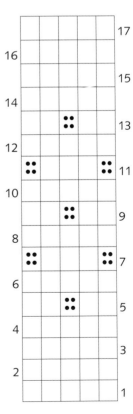

GIANT MESH SEQUIN BRACELET

A larger hook creates a lovely open lacy mesh. Add giant multi-coloured star sequins for a really pretty and unusual bracelet. The fabric is too loose for a popper. Instead, join the ends to make a complete ring. This open mesh has lots of stretch so it will easily slide over your hand.

Thread 14 sequins onto the wire (you may not need all of these). Add one randomly placed sequin to every right side row.

PATTERN

Using a 6.50 mm hook, make a slip knot, leaving a 10 cm (4 in) tail.

Make 5ch.

1st Row (Wrong side) 1dc into 2nd ch from hook, 1dc into each ch to end, turn (4 sts).

2nd Row (Right side) Add one sequin placed randomly to this row. 1ch, 1dc into each st to end, turn.

3rd Row No sequin this row. 1ch, 1dc into each dc to end, turn.

Repeat 2nd and 3rd rows until bracelet fits comfortably around your wrist, ending with a right side row.

MAKING UP

Fold bracelet gently in half (without crushing) with right sides facing inwards. Join the two ends by working one row of ss across each st. Fasten off, weave in ends.

tubular necklace and bracelet

Dress to excess and relive the big-shouldered power-dressing chic of the eighties with this tubular jewellery in colour-lights yarn! This necklace in red sparkly yarn and tipped with beads, looks great snaked around the neck. It's very simple to make, worked in a spiral without increases or decreases.

SKILL Easy

TUBE NECKLACE

MATERIALS
1 x 25g ball of Anchor Arista shade 328
60 cm (23½ in of 18 gauge jewellery wire
Nylon thread
1 tube of Gutermann Rocaille 9 seed beads, shade 4740

EQUIPMENT
3.00 mm crochet hook
Blunt-ended needle
Round-nosed pliers
Scissors

SIZE
This can be made to any size, measure against your neck as you go.

PATTERN
Leaving a 20 cm (7¾ in) tail, make a slip knot.
Make 6ch, join in a ring with a ss.
1st round Work 10dc into centre of ring.
2nd round 1dc into each dc to end.
Repeat 2nd round until necklace fits comfortably around your neck and overlaps by at least 10 cm (4 in). It doesn't matter if you have not reached the end of the round. After the first couple of rounds, you

won't be able to keep track of where the round begins and ends, and in any case, it won't show [see above]. Fasten off leaving a 20 cm (7¾ in) tail.

FINISHING
Using the tail, sew up one of the ends firmly so that the wire will not be able to poke through. Using the pliers, fold over the ends of the wire to create a rounded end and feed it into the necklace. Now sew up the other end.

Using nylon thread, as it is all but invisible, sew the beads onto each end of the necklace in an irregular pattern, applying two at a time. Sew in all ends.

Gently manipulate the wired tube to fit around your neck.

TUBE BRACELET

MATERIALS

1 x 25g ball of Anchor Arista, shade 332

15 cm (6 in) of 1mm jewellery wire

EQUIPMENT

As for tube necklace

SIZE

This can be made to any size, measure against your wrist as you go.

PATTERN

Leaving a 20 cm (7¾ in) tail, make a slip knot.

Make 5ch, join in a ring with a ss.

1st round Work 8dc into centre of ring.

2nd round 1dc into each dc to end.

Repeat 2nd round until bracelet just fits around your wrist. Fasten off leaving a 20 cm (7¾ in) tail.

MAKING UP

Using the tail, sew up one of the ends firmly so that the wire will not be able to poke through. Using the pliers, fold over the ends of the wire to create a rounded end and feed it into the bracelet. Now sew up the other end. Sew in all ends.

> **tip**
> It is quite easy to miss or add a stitch. So make sure you count your stitches regularly to save having to undo your work.

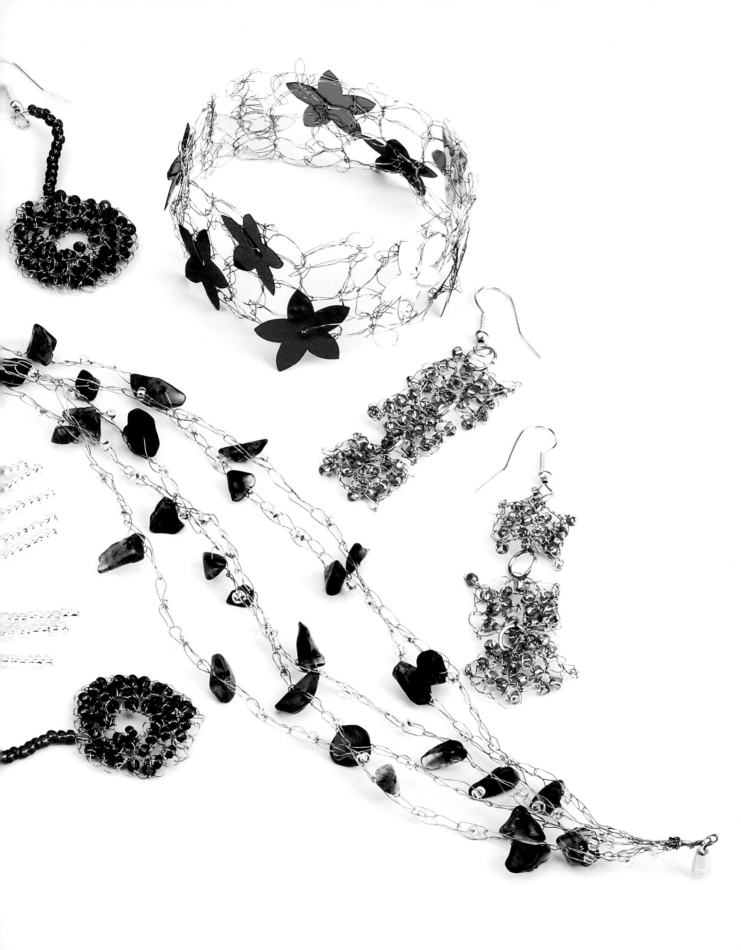

multicoloured bead ring

A cool band ring in multicoloured hues with beads worked into both sides of the fabric. So easy, it only takes minutes to make.

SKILL Easy

MATERIALS
1 tube of multicoloured 5 mm glass beads
1 reel of 32 gauge silver jewellery wire

EQUIPMENT
3.00 mm crochet hook
Scissors

SIZES – SMALL, MEDIUM, LARGE
Instructions for the smaller size are given first, larger sizes are in brackets.

special term
Dcb This is one double crochet with a bead. To work a bead into the fabric, slide the bead up the wire so it is close to the fabric, insert hook to the left of the bead and into the next stitch, yrh, draw through a loop, yrh, draw through two loops. The bead will now be caught in the stitch.

PREPARATION
Thread on 36 (39, 42) multicoloured beads in any order.

PATTERN
Make a slip knot.
Make 4ch.
1st Row 1dcb into 2nd ch from hook, 1dcb into each of next 2ch, turn (3 sts).
2nd Row 1ch, 1dcb into each st to end, turn.
Repeat 2nd row until the band just fits around your finger. Do not fasten off.

MAKING UP
As the beads are on both sides of the mesh, there is no right or wrong side. Carefully fold the band in half so that the two ends are aligned. Work one row of ss across the ends. Fasten off. Weave in all ends.

gold chain belt

This stunning gold chain belt uses a very simple technique called double chain, with pendant beads worked in. Finished with a hook it can be worn as tight or loose as you like.

SKILL medium

MATERIALS
1 x 25 g ball of Twilleys Goldfingering in gold, shade 4
25 g of large mixed glass beads, red
Small hook (of hook-and-eye set)

EQUIPMENT
2.50 mm crochet hook
Round-nosed pliers

SIZES
Small: 96 cm (37¾ in) – actual length of belt
Medium/large: 115 cm (46 in)

special term
Dch Double chain. Start by making a double crochet, *insert hook under left loop of the stitch you have just made, yrh and draw through a loop, yrh, draw through two loops; this is one dch. Repeat from * until chain is required length.

PREPARATION – MAKING PENDANT BEADS

So that the beads hang nicely from the chain, instead of threading them directly onto the yarn, they will be suspended on a short length of wire.

For each bead, cut a piece of wire approximately 3 cm (1¾ in) length (you may need to use a shorter or

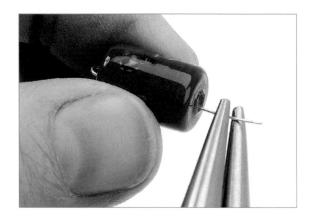

longer piece of wire depending on the size of your bead). Using a pair of round-nosed pliers, make a small loop at one end; this will ensure the bead doesn't slip off. Slip the bead onto the wire and at the other end make a slightly larger loop which the yarn will pass through. Poke the end of the wire back through the bead.

Thread on 25 (30) beads.

PATTERN
Make a slip knot, incorporating the first bead. Make 2ch.

1dc into 2nd chain from hook. Work 10dch, slide a bead up the yarn so it is close to your work. You might find it helpful to tuck it behind the work so that it doesn't get in the way. Continue to work 10dch, one bead, until you have reached the last bead. Work 10 more dch, fasten off.

MAKING UP

To complete the belt, simply sew a hook (from a hook-and-eye set) to the end of the belt. This can then be hooked anywhere along the length of the belt for a tight or relaxed look. Sew in any remaining ends.

tip

If you prefer, you can buy beads that already come in a wire cage with a loop for threading.

tumbling tendrils earrings

These striking and elegant earrings are made from tumbling tendrils of sparkly bronze yarn crocheted in differing length spirals. The spiral effect is created by increasing by the same amount into each stitch, forcing the fabric to create this fabulous twist.

SKILL Easy

MATERIALS
1 x 25 g ball of Arista Anchor, shade 314

1 pair of earring hooks

EQUIPMENT
2.50 mm crochet hook

Flat-nosed pliers

Blunt-ended needle

Scissors

PATTERN

FIRST TENDRIL
Make a slip knot.

Make 25ch.

Inserting hook into 4th ch from hook, work 3 tr. Work 4tr into each ch to last ch but one.

SECOND TENDRIL
Without fastening off, make 30ch.

Inserting hook into 4th ch from hook, work 3tr. Work 4tr into each ch to 2nd ch from end, work 1tr, 1htr, 1dc, 1ss into next ch, leaving last ch unworked.

MAKING UP
Fasten off and sew in the ends. Attach an earring hook to the centre of the two tendrils. You may need to use a pair of pliers to open and firmly close the connecting ring on the earring hook.

tip
Always insert the hook under 2 strands of the base chain and make sure the base chain doesn't get twisted as this will create a slightly uneven look.

swirl brooch with pompoms

This cute brooch would look great worn on a coat or jacket for a new take on the wintry pompom. The swirl brooch is made by working lots of increases which create this amazing texture.

SKILL Easy

MATERIALS
1 x 50 g ball of Rowan RYC Cashsoft dk in Lime
A piece of cardboard 10 cm x 5 cm (4 in x 2 in) for
   the pompoms
Silver brooch bar
Strong craft glue

EQUIPMENT
4.00 mm crochet hook
Blunt-ended needle
Scissors

BROOCH
Make a slip knot.
Make 6ch, join in a ring with a ss.
1st Round Work 15dc into ring.
2nd Round 3ch (count as 1tr), 2tr into base of 3ch, 3tr into each dc, ending with a ss into top of 3ch (45 sts)
3rd Round 3ch (count as 1tr), 2tr into base of 3ch, 3tr into each tr, ending with a ss into top of 3ch (135 sts).
4th Round As 3rd round (405 sts). Fasten off.

POMPOMS – MAKE 2
Cut 2 identical discs of cardboard measuring 5 cm (2 ins) diameter. Cut a 2 cm (¾ in) diameter hole in the centre of both discs.

Place the discs together and passing the yarn through the centre of the hole, wrap the yarn around the outside of the discs. You will not be able to get the whole ball through the centre of the disc, so cut off a length of yarn, wind this into a small ball and work with that. You can always add more yarn if you need it. When the cardboard is generously covered (so that it has a padded look) cut the yarn at the edge of the discs. Take a piece of yarn 50 cm (19½ ins) long and leaving one short tail and one long, wrap it very tightly around the cut pieces in between the two discs and tie a knot. Remove the cardboard discs and fluff out your pompom.

Make a slip knot as close as you can to the pompom. Make 15 chains. Fasten off.

MAKING UP
Attach both pompoms to the swirl brooch. Sew in all ends. Using strong craft glue, fix the brooch bar to the back of the swirl.

sparkly flower corsage

A fabulous flower corsage in contrasting sparkly yarns, worked with two sets of petals for an amazing three-dimensional look.

SKILL Medium

MATERIALS
1 x 25 g ball of Twilleys Goldfingering in pink, shade 59

1 x 25 g ball of Twilleys Goldfingering in black, shade 31

10 mm (¾ in) brooch bar

EQUIPMENT
2.50 mm crochet hook

Blunt-ended needle

Strong craft glue

Scissors

special terms
Flo: Front loop only. Work the stitch in the normal way, but inserting the hook under the front loop only of each st.

Blo: Back loop only. Work the stitch in the normal way, but inserting the hook under the back loop only of each st.

PATTERN
Work the central part of the flower in a spiral – this is a quicker way of working, but you will need to count your stitches as you go, or place a piece of yarn to mark the beginning of the row.

Using the black yarn, make a slip knot.
Make 2ch.

1st Round (Right side) work 8dc in 2nd ch from hook.

2nd Round 2dc into each dc to end. (16 sts)

3rd Round *1dc into next dc, 2dc into next dc; rep from * to end of round (24 sts).

4th Round *1dc into each of next 2dc, 2dc into next dc; rep from * to end of round (32 sts).

5th Round *1dc into each of next 3dc, 2dc into next dc; rep from * to end of round (40 sts).
Do not fasten off.

With right side facing, attach the pink yarn into the front loop of the next st.

FRONT PETALS
To make the front set of petals work into the front loop only of each st.

1st Row 1dc flo into each of the next 7 sts, turn.

2nd Row 1ch, 1dc into each dc to end, turn.

3rd Row 1ch, 2dctog, 1dc into each dc to end, turn.
Repeat 3rd row until 1 st remains, turn.

Next row 1ch, 1dc into remaining dc.
Working down the left side of the petal (right side facing), 1dc into each row end (8 sts), ss flo into next st.
Make four more petals as the first.

BACK PETALS
Using the pink yarn, ss across the back of the next 4 sts.

1st Row 1dc into the back loop only of each of the next 7 sts, turn.

2nd and 3rd Rows 1ch, 1dc into each dc to end, turn.

4th Row 1ch, 2dctog, 1dc into each dc to end, turn.

Repeat 4th row until 2 sts remain, turn.

Next row 1ch, 1dc into each dc to end, turn.

Next row 1ch, 2dctog, turn.

Next row 1ch, 1dc into remaining dc.

Working down the left side of each petal, 1dc into each row end (10 sts), ss blo into next st.

Make four more petals as the first.

BLACK BORDER FOR FRONT PETALS

Attach the black yarn to the ss in between two front petals.

Working up the right side of the first petal, work into the row ends as follows: 1dc into end of 1st row, 2dc into end of next row, 2htr into end of next row, 2tr into end of next row, 2tr into end of next row, 2htr into end of next row, 2dc into end of next row, 2dc into end of next row. Now work into sts down other side of petal as follows: 1ch, 2dc into next st, 2dc into next st, 2htr into next st, 2tr into next st, 2tr into next st, 2htr into next st, 2dc into next st, 1dc into next st. Repeat for each petal. Fasten off.

BLACK BORDER FOR BACK PETALS

Attach the black yarn to the 2nd ss in between 2 back petals.

Working up the right side of the first petal, work into each row end as follows: 1dc into end of 1st row, 2dc into end of next row, 2htr into end of next row, 2tr into end of next row, 2tr into end of next row, 2tr into end of next row, 2htr into end of next row, 2dc into end of next row, 2dc into end of next row, 1dc into end of next row. Now work into sts down other side of petal as follows: 1ch, 2dc into next st, 2dc into next st, 2htr into next st, 2tr into next st, 2tr into next st, 2tr into next st, 2htr into next st, 2dc into next st, 2dc into next st, 1dc into next st.

Repeat for each petal. Ss into next st. Fasten off.

MAKING UP

Attach the brooch bar with a dab of glue or secure with the ends. Sew in all ends.

love heart earrings

These funky heart-shaped earrings are very simple to make, using only very small quantities of yarn and finished with a round of sparkling beads. So quick and simple, you'll be able to whiz them up in no time at all for a night out.

SKILL Easy

MATERIALS

1 x 25 g ball of Twilleys Goldfingering, shade 59

1 tube of Gutermann Rocaille 9 seed beads, shade 4965

1 reel of 32 gauge silver jewellery wire

1 pair of earring hooks

EQUIPMENT

2.50 mm crochet hook

Blunt-ended needle

Scissors

special term

Dcb This is one double crochet with a bead. To work a bead into the fabric, slide the bead up the yarn so it is close to the fabric, insert hook to the left of the bead and into the next stitch, yrh, draw through a loop, yrh, draw through two loops. The bead will now be caught in the stitch.

PATTERN

Using the Goldfingering and 2.50 mm crochet hook, make a slip knot.

Make 17ch.

1st Row 1dc in 2nd ch from hook and in each of next 6ch, miss 2ch, 1dc into each of next 7ch, turn (14 sts).

2nd Row 1ch, 2dc in 1st dc, 1dc in each of next 5dc, miss 2ch, 1dc in each of next 5dc, 2dc in last dc, turn.

3rd and 4th Rows As 2nd row.

5th Row 1dc in each of next 6dc, miss 2dc, 1dc in each of next 6dc, turn (12 sts).

6th Row 1ch, dc2tog, 1dc in each of next 3dc, miss 2ch, 1dc in each of next 3dc, dc2tog.

BEAD EDGING

Thread the beads onto the wire before crocheting. You will need approx 38 beads for each earring.

Without turning, attach the wire into the next st, and work one round of dc around the heart as follows: 1dcb into each row end, 1dcb into the back of each ch, 3dcb into 2ch sp at the bottom centre, 1dcb into the back of each ch, 1dcb into each row end, 1dcb into each of next 4dc, miss 2dc, 1dcb into each of next 4dcb, ss into first dcb. Fasten off.

MAKING UP

Sew in ends and attach earring hook to the top centre of each heart.

stripy cuffs

Simple yet striking cuffs in two stripy variations. These are really simple to crochet and can be made to fit any wrist size. As one ball of each colour will make lots of cuffs, why not make a cuff for a friend?

SKILL Medium (both styles)

WAVE CUFF

MATERIALS

1 x 25 g ball of Twilleys Goldfingering in turquoise, shade 53

1 x 25 g ball of Twilleys Goldfingering in dark blue, shade 55

EQUIPMENT

3.00 mm crochet hook

2 small black hooks and eyes

Scissors

SIZES

Small: to fit wrists 15–17 cm (6–6¾ in)

Medium: to fit wrists 17–19 cm (6¾–7½ in)

Large: to fit wrists 19–21 cm (7½–8¼ in)

Instructions for the smallest size are given first, larger sizes are in brackets.

Start with the darker shade to give a better look and create a natural border. Alternate by working two rows in each shade. Change yarns during the last stitch in the row before the colour change, by working the last loop of the stitch before you need to change yarn, using the new yarn so the new colour is ready to be used for the turning chain.

PATTERN

Make a slip knot.

Make 44ch.

1st Row (right side) 1dc into 2nd ch from hook, *1dc into next ch, (1htr into next ch) twice, (1tr into next ch) twice, (1dtr into next ch) three times, (1tr into next ch) twice, (1htr into next ch) twice, (1dc into next ch) twice; rep from * to end, turn.

2nd Row 1ch, 1dc into each st to end, turn.

Change to other colour yarn.

3rd Row 4ch (count as 1dtr), miss 1st st, *1dtr into next st, (1tr into next st) twice, (1htr into next st) twice, (1dc into next st) 3 times, (1htr into next st) twice, (1tr into next st) twice, (1dtr into next st) twice; rep from * to end, turn.

4th Row 1ch, 1dc into each st to end, working last dc into top of tch, turn.

Change back to first colour of yarn.

5th Row 1ch, 1dc into first st, *1dc into next st, (1htr

into next st) twice, (1tr into next st) twice, (1dtr into next st) three times, (1tr into next st) twice, (1htr into next st) twice, (1dc into next st) twice; rep from * to end, turn.

6th Row 1ch, 1dc into each st to end, turn.

Repeat 3rd to 6th rows. Don't fasten off.

MAKING UP

FOR SMALL SIZE ONLY

1ch, without turning, work one round of dc evenly around three sides of the cuff, working 3dc into each corner.

MEDIUM AND LARGE SIZES

Work one round of dc around three sides of the cuff, working extra rows of dc at row-end edge as follows:
**1st Row 1ch, 1dc into each row end, turn.
2nd Row 1ch, 1dc into each dc to end, turn.

MEDIUM ONLY

3rd Row 1ch, 1dc into each dc to last dc, 3dc in last dc, don't turn.

LARGE ONLY

Repeat 2nd row twice more
Next row 1ch, 1dc into each dc to last dc, 3dc in last dc, don't turn. **

MEDIUM AND LARGE Continue to work around the cuff, working 1dc into the back of each ch until you reach the last ch, 3dc in last ch.

Repeat from ** to ** once more.

ALL SIZES

> ### tip
> Remember to insert the crochet hook under both strands of the base chain when working a stitch. This will create a firm and even edge.

Fasten off, sew in all ends. Now attach two hooks evenly at one end of the cuff and attach two eyes in corresponding positions at the other end.

ZIGZAG CUFF

MATERIALS

1 x 25 g ball of Twilleys Goldfingering in light grey, shade 57
1 x 25 g ball of Twilleys Goldfingering in purple, shade 60

EQUIPMENT

3.00 mm crochet hook
2 small black hooks and eyes
Scissors

SIZES

Small: to fit wrists 15–17 cm (6–6¾ in)
Medium: to fit wrists 17–19 cm (6¾–7½ in)
Large: to fit wrists 19–21 cm (7½–8¼ in)

Instructions for the smallest size are given first, larger sizes are in brackets.

Alternate colours by working two rows in each shade. For tips on changing yarn, see wave cuff.

PATTERN

Make a slip knot.
Make 57ch.
1st Row 2dc into 2nd ch from hook, *1dc into each of next 4ch, miss 2ch, 1dc into each of next 4ch, 3dc into next ch; rep from * ending last repeat with just 2dc in the last ch, turn.
2nd Row 1ch, 2dc into 1st st, *1dc into each of next 4 sts, miss 2 sts, 1dc into each of next 4 sts, 3dc into next st; rep from * ending last repeat with just 2dc in the last st, turn.
Change to other colour yarn.
Repeat 2nd row eight times more, working two rows

pretty in pink choker

You shall go to the ball! A gorgeous choker with rows of pink beads, and threaded through with satin ribbons that tie at the back.

SKILL Medium

MATERIALS

1 x 10 g ball of DMC Coton Perlé 5, shade 761

160 cm (63 in) of 6 mm (¼ in) pink satin ribbon

1 tube of Gutermann satin Rocaille 9, shade 4395

EQUIPMENT

2.50 mm crochet hook

Blunt-ended needle

Collapsible-eye beading needle

SIZE

Small: to fit neck size 30–35 cm (11¾–13¾ in)

Medium/large: to fit neck size 36–40 cm (14–15¾ in)

Instructions for the smaller size are given first; the larger size is in brackets.

Thread 50 cm (55 cm), 19½ in (21½ in) of beads or 210 (222) beads.

PATTERN

Make 73 (77) ch.

1st Row Work 1dc into 2nd ch from hook, 1dc into each ch to end, turn. 72 (76) sts

2nd Row 1ch, 1dc into first st, 1dcb into each dc to last dc, 1dc into last dc, turn.

3rd Row 1ch, 1dc into each st to end, turn.

4th Row 3ch, miss first dc, 1tr into each of next 5dc, *1ch, miss 1dc, 1tr into next dc; rep from * to last 6 sts, 1tr into each of next 6dc, turn.

special terms

Dtr (double treble) Wrap the yarn round the hook twice, insert hook into the work, yrh, draw a loop through the work, yrh, draw through first two loops on hook, yrh, draw through the next two loops on the hook, yrh, draw through the last two loops on the hook. You will be left with one loop on the hook.

Dcb This is one double crochet with a bead. To work a bead into the fabric, slide the bead up the yarn so it is close to the work, insert the hook into the next st, yrh, draw through a loop, yrh, draw through two loops [see above].

5th Row 1ch, 1dc into each tr and each ch sp to end, working last dc into top of tch, turn.
Repeat 2nd to 5th rows once more.
Repeat 2nd to 3rd rows once more. Fasten off.

MAKING UP

Cut the ribbon in half and thread each half onto a needle. Starting with the ribbon at the back, weave in and out of the spaces. Place a small dab of glue or nail varnish on the ends of the ribbon so that they don't fray.

flower hair slides

You can make lots of these pretty hair slides in different colour combinations – they are so quick and easy.

SKILL Easy

MATERIALS

DMC Coton Perlé 5 point, shades 211, 962, 3326 and 899

Hair slides

Strong craft glue

Large star sequins (1 per slide)

EQUIPMENT

2.00 mm crochet hook

Needle

Scissors

PATTERN

Using colour A (any colour), make 5ch, join in a ring with a ss.

1st Round 1ch, work 10dc into ring, ss into first dc.

2nd Round 1ch, 2dc into each dc, ss into first dc (20 sts).

3rd Round 2ch, working into the front loop only *1tr into each of next 3dc, 2ch, ss into next st; rep from * four more times working last ss into base of first 2ch. (Five petals made.) Fasten off.

Working into the back loop only, attach colour B (any colour, not A) into the back loop of first dc, *3ch, 2dtr into each of next 3dc, 3ch, ss into next dc; rep from * four more times, working last ss into base of first 3ch. Fasten off.

special terms

Flo Front loop only. Work the stitch in the normal way, but inserting the hook under the front loop only of each st.

Blo Back loop only. Work the stitch in the normal way, but inserting the hook under the back loop only of each st [See picture above].

Dtr (double treble) Wrap the yarn round the hook twice, insert hook into the work, yrh, draw a loop through the work, yrh, draw through first two loops on hook, yrh, draw through the next two loops on the hook, yrh, draw through the last two loops on the hook. You will be left with one loop on the hook.

MAKING UP

Sew in all the ends and press the flower flat. Now slide onto the hair slide. Attach the sequin to the centre of the flower with a small dab of glue.

berry bead earrings

Pretty pendant earrings worked in a swirl of berry coloured beads. They are made using only the most basic techniques and are an easy project for a beginner to undertake.

SKILL Easy

MATERIALS

1 tube of Gutermann Rocaille 9 seed beads, shade 5435

1 x reel of 32 gauge silver jewellery wire

1 pair of earring hooks

EQUIPMENT

2.00 mm crochet hook

Flat-nose pliers

Scissors

special term

Dcb This is one double crochet with a bead. To work a bead into the fabric, slide the bead up the wire so it is close to the fabric, insert hook to the left of the bead and into the next stitch, yrh, draw through a loop, yrh, draw through two loops. The bead will now be caught in the stitch.

PATTERN

Thread on 48 beads for each earring.

Make a slip knot.

Make 2ch.

1st Round Work 8dcb into 2nd ch from hook.

2nd Round 2dcb into each st (16 sts).

3rd Round * 1dcb into next st, 2dcb into next st; rep from * to end, ss into 1st dcb (24 sts). Fasten off leaving a 10 cm (4 in) tail.

MAKING UP

Thread 15 beads onto the tail, thread the tail through the ring on the bottom of the earring hook, wrap the wire back round itself to secure and pass through the next couple of beads. Cut the wire close to the beads.

tip
When finishing these earrings off, take care not to
overstress the wire it may break.

daisy chain necklace

Delicate white and yellow daisies that can be worked up very quickly are linked with jump rings and finished with a clasp for a new crocheted take on a traditional theme.

SKILL Easy

MATERIALS
1 skein of DMC Mouliné 25, shade 445
1 reel of DMC Coton Perlé 5 point, in white
10 (11) round silver jump rings
1 barrel clasp

EQUIPMENT
3.00 mm crochet hook
Blunt-ended needle
Flat-nosed pliers
Scissors

TENSION
Each flower should measure 3.5 cm (1¼ in) from tip to tip. The flowers do not need to be exactly this size, but you should ensure they are all the same size as each other to achieve a uniform look.

SIZE
Small: to fit neck size 30–35 cm (11¾–13¾ in)
Medium/large: to fit neck size 36–40 cm (14–15¾ in)
Instructions for smaller size are first; larger is in brackets

PATTERN
Make 11 (12) flowers.
Using the yellow yarn, make a slip knot.
Make 2ch.
1st Round Work 5dc into 2nd ch from hook.

special terms

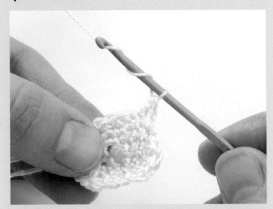

Dtr (double treble) Wrap the yarn round the hook twice [see above], insert hook into the work, yrh, draw a loop through the work, yrh, draw through first two loops on hook, yrh, draw through the next two loops on the hook, yrh, draw through the last two loops on the hook. You will be left with one loop on the hook.

2nd Round 2dc into each dc to end (10 sts).
3rd Round Using the white yarn,*1dc into next st, 2dc into next st; rep from* to end (15 sts).
4th Round *2ch, 1tr into first dc, 1dtr into next dc, 1tr into next dc, 2ch, ss into next dc; rep from * four more times, working ss at end of last repeat into base of 2ch at beg of round. Fasten off.

MAKING UP

Sew in all the ends. Press the flowers so they are flat.
Using a pair of flat-nosed pliers, open a jump ring and
thread it through the top of the dtr on any two petals
of two flowers. Close the ring. Continue until all the
daisies are linked into a chain.

tip

When changing colour, introduce the new colour
into the last loop of the stitch before the actual
colour change.

silver chain anklet

A sexy summer ankle chain in a sparkly silver yarn with drop beads and fastened with a barrel clasp. This is very quick to make and only uses a tiny amount of yarn and beads.

SKILL Easy

MATERIALS
1 x 25 g ball of Twilleys Goldfingering in silver, shade 5
7 (small) or 8 (medium/large) beads
1 barrel clasp

EQUIPMENT
2.5 mm crochet hook
Collapsible-eye beading needle
Blunt-ended needle
Scissors

SIZE
Small: 19 cm (7½ in)
Medium/large: 22 cm (8½ in)
Instructions for the smaller size are first, instructions for medium/large are in brackets.

special term
Picot Make 3ch, ss into 3rd chain from hook.

PREPARATION – MAKING PENDANT BEADS
So that the beads hang nicely from the chain, instead of threading them directly onto the yarn, they will be suspended on a short length of wire.

For each bead, cut a piece of wire approximately 3 cm (¾ in) in length (you may need to use a shorter or longer piece of wire depending on the size of your bead). Using a pair of round-nosed pliers, make a small loop at one end – this will ensure the bead doesn't slip off. Thread the bead onto the wire and at the other end make a slightly larger loop, which will pass through. Poke the end of the wire back through the bead.

If you prefer, you can buy beads that already come in a wire cage with a loop for threading.

Thread on 7 (8) beads.

PATTERN

Make a slip knot.

Make 45 (51) ch.

1st Row Work 1dc into 2nd ch from hook, 1dc into each ch to end, turn. 44 (50) sts.

2nd Row 5ch, miss first 3dc, 1dc into next dc, work 1 picot, 1dc into next dc, *5ch, miss 4dc, 1dc into next dc, work 1 picot, 1dc into next dc; rep from * to last 3dc, 2ch, miss 2 dc, 1tr into last dc, turn.

3rd Row 1ch, 1dc into first tr, *8ch, 1dc into next 5ch arch; rep from * to end working last dc into 3rd of 5ch, turn.

4th Row 1ch, 1dc into first dc, *(5dc, slide a bead up, 5dc) into next 8ch arch, 1dc into next dc; rep from * to end. Fasten off.

MAKING UP

Press the anklet carefully avoiding the beads. Sew in all ends. Attach barrel clasp to each end of 1st row.

dangly squares earrings

These pretty earrings are created simply by making three small wire mesh squares for each earring with delicate pink seed beads worked in. The squares are then linked together with small rings so that they hang.

SKILL Medium

MATERIALS

1 x tube of Gutermann Rocaille 9 seed beads, shade 4965

1 reel of 32 gauge silver jewellery wire

1 pair of earring hooks

6 round silver jump rings

Strong craft glue

EQUIPMENT

Flat-nosed pliers

2.00 mm crochet hook

Scissors

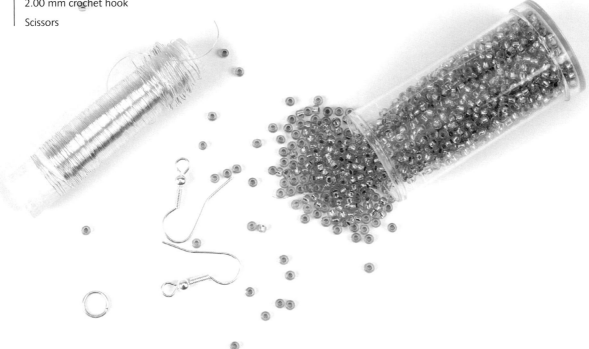

PREPARATION

First, thread on 48 beads for each earring. These are all the beads you will need for each earring, though it may be worth adding a few more in case you have miscounted.

PATTERN

Make a slip knot.

Make 5ch.

1st Row 1dcb into 2nd ch from hook, 1dcb into each ch to end, turn (4 sts).

2nd Row 1ch, 1dcb into each dcb to end, turn.

3rd and 4th Rows As 2nd row. Fasten off.

Make another 5 mesh squares in this way.

MAKING UP

To make up each earring: weave the wire ends into the mesh and cut. Attach each of the squares with a centrally placed jump ring. You may need to use the pliers to open and close the rings. Now add a ring to the top centre of the top square and attach the earring hook.

tip

As the wire is very fine, and may easily work its way through the gap in the jump rings, seal the rings with a dab of glue applied with a pin.

Furry scrunchies

These scrunchies are so easy and super speedy to make and look great in this funky fake fur yarn. One ball will makes lots of scrunchies, so go wild!

SKILL Very easy

MATERIALS

1 x 50 g ball of Patons Whisper in shades Bloom, Gem and Jet

1 hair band for each scrunchy

EQUIPMENT

4.00 mm crochet hook

Blunt-ended needle

Scissors

PATTERN

Hold the hair band in front of the yarn, between the thumb and middle finger of your left hand. Insert the hook into the middle of the band, yrh, draw the hook back through the band, yrh, draw through the loop on the hook.

Insert the hook into the band once more, yrh, draw the hook through the band, yrh, draw the hook through both loops on the hook; this will leave one loop. This makes one double crochet.

4ch (count as 1tr and 1ch), *1tr, 1ch; rep from * all the way around the band until it is no longer visible even when stretched out. Ss into top of 4ch. Cut the end, and draw the tail through the final loop. Sew in both ends.

two-tone ring bangles

This project is one of the quickest in the book – taking only minutes to make. This elegant and chic bracelet in two tones of yarn is worked in double crochet around a series of small rings.

SKILL Easy

MATERIALS
6 or 7 x 25 mm brass rings (curtain accessories)
1 skein each of Anchor Mouliné, shades 102 and 108

EQUIPMENT
2.50 mm crochet hook
Blunt-ended needle
Scissors

SIZE
Smal: to fit wrists 15–18 cm (6–7 in) – use 6 rings
Medium/large: to fit 18–21 cm (7–8¼ in) – use 7 rings

TENSION
Although tension is not important for this pattern, the stitches should be fairly tight and fit snugly around the ring.

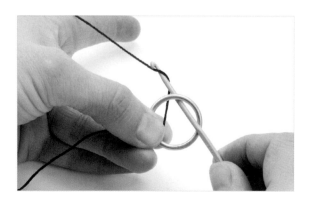

PATTERN

Using shade 108, hold the yarn in your left hand in the normal way. You will also need to hold the first ring between the thumb and middle finger of your left hand. Insert the hook into the ring from front to back, yrh, draw the loop back through the ring, yrh, and draw through the loop on the hook [see bottom left].

Insert the hook into the ring, yrh, draw loop back through the ring, yrh, draw hook through both loops on the hook, this will leave one loop. This makes one double crochet.

Work a further 15dc into the centre of the ring. Now add a new ring. Holding the new ring in your left hand between your thumb and middle finger, insert the hook into this new ring, yrh, draw the loop back through the ring, yrh, draw through both loops on hook. This is 1dc.

Work a further 15dc into the 2nd ring. Continue in this way, working 16dc around each new ring. On the final ring, change yarn after the first 16dc and using shade 102 work a further 16dc, ending with a ss into the first dc on that ring.

Now ss into the final dc on the previous ring, and work 16dc around that ring, ending with a ss into the first dc on that ring.

Continue to work 16 more dc around each ring ending with a ss into first dc of each ring until you are back at the first ring, ending with a ss into the first dc

on that ring. Join the bracelet into a ring by working a slip stitch into stitches 16 and 17 on the final ring. Fasten off. Sew in all ends.

Make a bigger impact by using two really contrasting colours, rather than two shades of the same one. Try black and white, as shown here, for example.

floribunda barrette

A cornucopia of brightly coloured flowers on a leafy background make a striking hair accessory that is very simple and quick to make.

SKILL Easy

MATERIALS
1 skein each of DMC Mouliné 25 thread, shades 608, 603, 321, and 909
1 plain barrette approx 7 cm (2¾ in) in length
Strong craft glue

EQUIPMENT
3.00 mm crochet hook
Blunt-ended tapestry needle
Scissors

FLOWERS
These flowers are very simply worked in a spiral and each take only a few minutes to make. Using shades 608, 603, and 321, make 7 flowers.

Make a slip knot.
Make 2ch.
1st Round Work 8 dc into 2nd ch from hook.
2nd Round 2tr into each dc to end. (16 sts).
3rd Round Miss first 2tr, 1dc around stem of next 8tr, 1dc around stem of each of next 2dc in row below, ss around stem of next dc. Fasten off.

LEAFY BACKGROUND
If your barrette is a different size to the one suggested in this pattern, you make need any multiple of four more or fewer chain stitches to start with, bearing in mind the base will stretch up to 1 cm (½ in) in length.

Make a slip knot.
Using DMC shade 909, make 15ch.
1st Round Work 1dc into 2nd ch from hook, 1dc into each ch to last ch, work 3dc into last ch. Now working into the back of the base ch, work 1dc into each ch to end, work 2dc into first ch of 2ch, ss into 2nd ch of 2ch (32 sts).
2nd Round 2ch, 3tr into first dc, 3dtr into next st, 3tr into next st, (1htr, 1dc) into next st, *3tr into next st, 3dtr into next st, 3tr into next st, (1htr, 1dc) into next st; repeat from * to end, ss into top of 2ch.
Fasten off.

MAKING UP

Using a crochet hook, draw the tails of the flowers through the leafy background from front to back, and tie the tails in a knot to secure the flowers. Sew in the ends. Remember you will not see the back of the leafy background. Now glue the background to the barrette.

boho beads

Boho beads are crocheted balls. For a great bohemian look, string the balls to make a necklace or bracelet. You can even mix them with glass beads. Make it short or long, multicoloured – whatever you like!

SKILL Easy

NECKLACE – LARGE BEADS

MATERIALS

1 x 50 g ball of Rowan Cotton Glace in Excite

1 tube of Gutermann 8 mm glass beads, shade 1000

Small bag of polyester filling or cotton wool

1 barrel clasp

2 crimps

EQUIPMENT

3.50 mm crochet hook

Flat-nosed pliers

Blunt-ended needle

Scissors

TENSION

Each ball should measure 3 cm (1¼ in) diameter or at least be of a uniform size.

PATTERN

For a short necklace interspersed with beads and finished with a clasp, make 12 balls. For a longer necklace that fits over the head, make at least 24 balls.
Make a slip knot.
Make 2ch.
1st Round Work 8dc into 2nd ch from hook.
2nd Round 2dc into each dc to end (16 sts).
3rd Round *1dc into each of the next 3dc, 2dc into next dc; rep from * to end (20 sts).
4th Round 1 dc into each dc to end.
5th Round *1dc into each of next 3dc, dc2tog into next dc; rep from * to end (16 sts).
Place filling into the ball.
6th Round Dc2tog 8 times (8 sts).
7th Round 1dc into each dc to end.
Fasten off. Sew in ends.

FINISHING

Using a sharp needle, thread the crocheted balls, alternating with glass beads if you like. At each end, thread on a crimp and then the clasp, and take the thread back through the crimp. Using the pliers crush the crimp flat. This will hold the clasp in place. Trim off any excess thread.

If you are making your necklace long enough to fit over your head, you may decide not to have a clasp. In that case simply thread the beads onto a piece of sturdy cotton thread and tie the ends firmly. Conceal the ends within the balls.

> **tip**
> These balls are a good way of using up odds and ends of yarn, though different yarns may make different sized balls.

BRACELET – SMALL BEADS

MATERIALS
1 x 50 g ball of Rowan Cotton Glace in Tickle
Small bag of polyester filling or cotton wool
Shirring elastic

EQUIPMENT
3.5 mm crochet hook
Blunt-ended needle
Scissors

TENSION
Each ball should measure 2.5 cm (1 in) diameter using a
3.50 mm hook. Although it doesn't matter what size your
beads are, you should ensure they are all the same size for
a neat and uniform look.

SIZES
Small: to fit wrists 15–17 cm (6–6¾ in)
Medium: to fit wrists 17–19 cm (6¾–7½ in)
Large: to fit wrists 19–21 cm (7½–8¼ in)

Instructions for the smallest size are given first, larger
sizes are in brackets.

PATTERN
Make 11 (13, 15) balls.
Make a slip knot.
Make 2ch.
1st Round Work 8dc into 2nd ch from hook.
2nd Round 2dc into each dc to end (16 sts).
3rd and 4th Rounds 1dc into each dc to end.
Place filling into the ball.
5th Round Dc2tog 8 times (8 sts).
6th Round 1dc into each dc to end.
Fasten off. Sew in ends.

Using a sharp needle, thread the beads onto the
elastic. Cut the elastic and tie a knot. Sew in the ends.

tip
As you are working in a spiral rather than complete
rounds, you should mark the beginning of each
round with a piece of coloured thread to avoid
losing your place.

suppliers

UK

Coats Crafts UK
PO Box 22
Lingfield House
Lingfield Point
McMullen Road
Darlington
County Durham DL1 1YQ
Tel: 01325 394237
www.coatscrafts.co.uk

Colinette Yarns
Banwy Workshops,
Llanfair Caereinion,
Powy, Wales
SY21 0SG
United Kingdom
Tel: 01938 810128
Fax: 01938 810127
www.colinette.com

DMC
Visit www.dmc.com for a full list of stockists

Perivale-Gütermann Ltd
Bullsbrook Road
Middlesex
UB4 0JR
www.guetermann.com

Rowan Yarns
Green Mill Lane
Holmfirth
West Yorkshire
HD 2DX
Tel: 01484 681 881
www.knitrowan.com

Twilleys of Stamford
Roman Mill
Stamford
Lincolnshire
PE9 1BG
Tel: 01780 752661
Fax: 01780 765215
www.tbramsden.co.uk

John Lewis
Oxford Street
London
W1A 1EX
Tel: 020 7629 7711
www.johnlewis.com

FRANCE

Elle Tricote
8 Rue de Coq
67000 Strasbourg
Tel: 00 33 88 23 03 13
www.elletricote.com

GERMANY

Designer Yarns
Handelsagentur Klaus Koch
Sachsstrasse 30
50259 Pulheim-Brauweiler
Tel: +49 (0) 2234 205453
www.designer-yarns.de

Coats GmbH,
Kaiserstr. 1, 79341 Kenzingen
Tel. +49 7644 802-287
www.coatsgmbh.de

SPAIN

Marian Artes De Arcos
Oyambre
Pan Claris 145
Barcelona
Spain

SWEDEN

Hamilton Designs
Langgatan 20
64730 Mariefred
Sweden
Tel: 00 46 159 12006
Fax: 00 46 159 12006
www.hamiltondesign.biz

BELGIUM

Pavan
Koningin Astridlaan 78
B9000 Gent
Tel: 32 9221 8594
Email: pavan@pandora.be

NEW ZEALAND

Knit world
Branches throughout New Zealand
www.knitting.co.nz
Tel: (04) 586 4530

Spotlight
Branches throughout New Zealand
www.spotlightonline.co.nz
Birch Haberdashery & Craft
8 Heremai Street
Henderson
Auckland
Tel: 09 8350466

Trendy Trims Ltd
7 Angle Street
Onehunga
Auckland
Tel: 096344531

AUSTRALIA

Sunspun
185 Canterbury Road
Canterbury
3126
Tel: (61) 3 5979 155
www.sunspun.com.au

Yarn Barn
Aaron Dickson
200 Reynard Street
Coburg Vic 3058
Tel: 03 9386 0361

Harmony Flowers
6 Doncaster Rd,
North Balwyn
VIC 3104
Melbourne
Tel: 03 9859 9859
www.harmonyflowers.com.au

SOUTH AFRICA

Arthur Bales
62, 4th Avenue
Linden
Johannesburg 2195
Tel: 011 888 2401

ABC Knitting & Haberdashery
327 President Street
Germiston 1401
Tel: 011 873 4296

Orion Wool Shop and Needlecraft
39 Adderley Street
Cape Town 8000
Tel: 021 461 6941

index